THE COMPLETE FOX

BY THE SAME AUTHOR

The Complete Hedgehog
Something in a Cardboard Box
The Hedgehog & Friends
The Complete Garden Bird
St Tiggywinkles Wildcare Handbook

ACKNOWLEDGEMENTS

I would like to thank Dr John Lewis,
of the International Zoo Veterinary Group, our
veterinary consultants, for his comments on the
medical content of *The Complete Fox*, and the
League Against Cruel Sports for permission to
quote extracts from Robert Churchward's 'A
Master of Hounds Speaks'. Also, once more,
Bucks and Herts Newspapers have supplied a
striking photograph (on p. 159).
Front cover photo, by Dennis Bright,
courtesy of the Swift Picture Library.

THE COMPLETE

FOX

LES STOCKER

Canterbury College

Drawings by Ian Coleman

Chatto & Windus
LONDON

First published 1994

1 3 5 7 9 10 8 6 4 2

Copyright © Les Stocker 1994
Photographs © Les Stocker
Drawings © Ian Coleman

First published in the United Kingdom in 1994 by
Chatto & Windus Limited
Random House, 20 Vauxhall Bridge Road,
London SW1V 2SA

Random House Australia (Pty) Limited
20 Alfred Street, Milsons Point, Sydney
New South Wales 2061, Australia

Random House New Zealand Limited
18 Poland Road, Glenfield
Auckland 10, New Zealand

Random House South Africa (Pty) Limited
PO Box 337, Bergvlei, South Africa

Random House UK Limited Reg. No. 954009

A CIP catalogue record for this book is available from the
British Library

ISBN 0 7011 3776 2

Design by Margaret Sadler

Printed and bound in Great Britain by
Butler & Tanner Ltd, Frome and London

CONTENTS

INTRODUCTION Fox, King of Beasts 1

CHAPTER 1 The Mud Sticks 14

CHAPTER 2 Foxes around their World 29

CHAPTER 3 About the Fox 50

CHAPTER 4 Living with Foxes 61

CHAPTER 5 'Tear 'im, Eat 'im' 76

CHAPTER 6 Casualty 92

CHAPTER 7 Intensive Care 110

CHAPTER 8 Young and Boisterous 126

CHAPTER 9 Genuine Orphans 137

CHAPTER 10 Back to the Wild 147

CHAPTER 11 Foxes and the Future 158

Useful Addresses 168

Bibliography 169

Index 170

INTRODUCTION

FOX, KING OF BEASTS

I had been travelling for miles along an ever decreasing track high in the Scottish Highlands. The tarmac had long since petered out as I put my hire car, a sleek Ford saloon, through its off-the-road paces. The hill had been bare of life: even the red stags had left the high ground to raid the sheep mangers around the farm that lay far behind me. An occasional buzzard mewed its despairing cry as it soared above me, vainly searching the heather for a scrap, a morsel to sustain it in this wilderness. There appeared to be nothing except brown heather, wounded occasionally by a cube of dark spruce, a Forestry Commission plantation. Mind you, this was the place to be, leaving all the noise and soot of the twentieth century far behind, and when the car finally stopped, the air was clear and quiet, and there was nothing but wilderness – I could as well have been in the foothills of the Himalayas, days from civilisation.

I soaked up the stillness. But then a red shadow deep in the valley below caught the corner of my eye. I grabbed my 'bins' and quickly focused on a majestic hill fox gliding between Forestry Commission plantations. His coat glowed and flowed in the mountain sunlight, and his brush streamed out behind him as he trotted through his domain. He looked strong and fit with not a blemish on that wonderful coat; this was obviously his kingdom, which he ruled with the majesty of the tiger in the Himalayas, or the lion in Africa. I was awed, privileged to have seen this superb wild animal in such spectacular surroundings.

Every time I see a fox it inspires a new superlative. Each animal is different, whether it is the supreme beast, like that hill fox, or the tiny fox cub that defied rescue from the rainwater tub it had fallen into. I meet many wild animals and regularly handle badgers, mink and fierce birds of prey, but somehow none, except perhaps the diminutive weasel who will readily threaten you, have had the courage of that soggy ball of spitting fury. Normally I have no hesitation in catching a fox cub rather as I would a cat, but as soon as I stuck my nose over the edge of the water butt and got hissed at, I knew that I could be in for trouble.

I always carry a thick stick that is known affectionately as a 'plonker', a genuine castoff from a group of Morris Men who onomatopoetically call the sticks used in their stick dances their 'plonkers'. I use mine not for dancing but as a protection against the jaws of badgers or large foxes, which can clamp onto the battered stick while I scruff them with my free hand. As I reached to the bottom of the tub the cub, a tiny vixen, stretched her jaws to latch onto my stick, giving me a moment to grab her scruff. She was dripping wet, but as I rubbed her dry with my free hand I made sure not to release my grip on her scruff or she would have tried to tear me apart. She weighed no more than a kitten but still demanded my whole attention.

Vixen cub trapped in a water butt and defying rescue

Judging by the food scattered around, her family were obviously living under the garden shed, so that's where I released her, although she still managed one turn and snap before she disappeared into the darkness to join her brothers and sisters.

Getting bitten should not be an occupational hazard if wildlife is handled properly, and in years of running a wildlife hospital I have learned to respect every animal for having quicker reflexes than I have. I never, ever give a fox the chance to bite, which it will instinctively do to defend itself. I am careful and never complacent, but I did get bitten once, luckily by a small fox who was barely out of nappies. He was obviously concentrating but I let my attention wander for an instant and nearly lost a finger.

About as big as a terrier dog, this cub had been spotted in the undergrowth at a school field centre. It was limping quite badly and trying to scavenge scraps from the school leftovers. When I arrived at the school, my heart fell at the excited audience of children who were set on not missing my attempts to waylay the fox. The animal had dozens of criss-crossing highways through the jungle of fallen trees and branches, and he constantly eluded my clumsy attempts to approach him. Deeper into the wood he led me until we were at last out of sight of the children. I realised that the best opportunity for catching him would be to drive him out into one of the open woodland glades and then outsprint him.

I only had my stick with which to handle him as foolishly I had left the net and carrying basket far behind me with the schoolchildren. There was nothing for it but to use my jacket and throw it over him if I managed to catch up with him on open ground.

At last he broke cover and, clumsy as I am, I still succeeded in outstripping him as he dragged that damaged leg. It was easy to throw my jacket over him, hold him with the stick and scruff him to carry him triumphantly back to the children and the carrying basket. But I had forgotten one thing: my jacket was still lying on the ground. With fox in one hand, I tried awkwardly to put it on. I soon had one arm safely ensconced in a sleeve – but, with the fox at arm's length, I still had to push my other, free arm through the empty sleeve and shrug the jacket onto my shoulder. I let my concentration slip for a second and my free hand popped out of the end of the empty sleeve exactly in front of the fox's nose. He clamped onto my finger in a trice, showing me that he was still the master.

The cub had serious damage to its hip but after a prolonged period of restricted cage rest it did recover and was released back into its undergrowth, this time without an audience of children, or a chance to bite unwary fingers.

All the foxes I have mentioned had the long, elegant, streamlined jaws of the fox family, but my first sight of a fox was of a skin with a silk lining and a hideous metal clip for its jaws, designed by pre-war fashion houses to grace some lady's neck. Where I grew up, in Battersea, South London, there were no real foxes then and very little other wildlife, except for the occasional hawk-moth caterpillars in the one lime tree on our street.

Since I lived within a stone's throw of Clapham Junction, I could take the train to the wilderness of Box Hill or Coulsdon, where the woods, which were full of spotted orchids, were my secret. I never saw a fox, nor even a sign of one, but I did see signs of other wild creatures: a skull, a feather, the occasional lizard, and once a majestic stag beetle that was lovingly carried back to 'The Den' at the bottom of the garden.

It was not a garden really but a high-walled yard with the remnants of an air-raid shelter, a vivid reminder of the bleak times. My mum had made a sort of garden out of the sooty soil, edged with empty scallop shells brought home by my father from his job as a fishmonger in Crouch End, across London. Post-war rationing kept necessities to a minimum so at the bottom of our 'garden' was a run of ramshackle chicken sheds that provided us with fresh eggs and, although I didn't know it at the time, a chicken at Christmas.

Later, the chicken sheds became my 'Den' where I could hide from my sisters and gloat over my wildlife collection. The stag beetle did not last long and even the lizard was carried off by somebody's pet jackdaw. My grass snake escaped, but my prize specimen, the fox, was safe. It was not a live fox but the silk-lined fox stole I had discovered in my gran's wardrobe. To me now it looks tatty and dull without the flow and colour of a live fox's coat and those

A young cub, alert and alive

cold, hard, glass eyes are nothing like the vibrant gold lights of a real fox's eyes. And then there were those jaws – a pathetic metal clip that clamped onto the lifeless brush. I didn't know any better and in those days nor did the world around me; the genesis of animal rights was still many years away.

Foxes went out of my mind after my schooldays as I enjoyed first the security of a career in accountancy and then the non-stop pressure of being in business for myself. I ended up in Buckinghamshire and eventually developed a small refrigeration engineering business. In the beginning I knew nothing about refrigeration engineering, but when a particular creditor defaulted I found myself in possession of numerous broken-down refrigerators. I took them apart and found out how to mend them. With a bit of lateral thinking, I came up with an equipment design that cut repair times by 75 per cent. This turned out to be a very valuable commodity which I hired to various manufacturers; I was then able to afford a holiday home in Dorset for the family, my wife Sue and our son Colin.

From then on our weekends were spent tramping the Purbeck Hills of Dorset, renewing all those reminiscences of my childhood treks across Box Hill. Just like then, Colin and I collected countryside bric-à-brac: feathers, pellets, fossils, shells and the frequent slow-worms which, now enlightened, we always released. One day we spotted four delightful fox cubs frolicking in the warm heathland air. We sat and watched, enchanted by the gambolling fights that I now know to be such an important part of fox adolescence. The following day they were gone and I never saw another live fox until some years later, after I had sold my business, when I came face to face with an adult fox in our kitchen.

I had become disenchanted with the cut and thrust of the business world. The obsession with all things wild that had haunted me as a boy was taking over again. Finally, as a family, together we made the decision to sell up and move to the coast, where I could try to earn a living by writing about that wild world which had gripped me again.

We never made it to the coast, but I did have the time to follow my instincts and make closer contact with the wildlife which had eluded me as a boy. At odd times during my office-bound years I had come across injured birds and, once even a hedgehog horribly infested with maggots. I lost them all, as apparently did everybody else who tried to look after sick or injured wildlife. But at least I could offer them a hospice in which to die quietly and in the warm, free from the terrors they must feel alone in the outside world.

Gradually, however, I discovered techniques to save some of these casualties. There were birds, frogs and even the occasional hedgehog; but until that fateful day when the RSPCA inspector produced a fox from his sack right in the middle of my kitchen, I had never had the privilege of meeting Britain's king of beasts.

I did not know which end to grab first. The fox did have a piece of rope, fashioned into a dog lead, around its neck but there any appearance of domestication ended. I had no idea what to do as it ran me around the kitchen. I struggled to put on a calm exterior, as I did not want the RSPCA inspector to know that this was the first fox I had ever handled.

'Give the inspector a cup of tea, Sue!' I hollered as I was dragged through the back door and into the garden, where I proceeded to do several laps of the perimeter fences. There was nowhere to put the fox as all my cages were small and my one aviary was quite frail and already housed a kestrel, Purdie, my first ever casualty. The garage! That was the answer, so I let him lead me in there. Somehow I got the rope off the fox's neck and set him free among all my paraphernalia, whilst I ran out, slammed the door, then calmly returned to the inspector for a cuppa, acting as though I had been handling foxes all my life.

When the inspector eventually left I crept back into the garage with bowls of water and dog food. Very, very warily I peeked through a gap in the door, but the fox knew I was there before I did. He was sitting on a pile of boxes, mouth slightly open, tongue lolling out of the side of it, defying me to make a wrong move. I dropped the bowls on the floor, quickly removed my arm before he could attach himself to it, and slammed the door well and truly shut.

A council of war with Sue followed, during which we tried to decide what to do with the fox and, in particular, where to house him. He did not seem injured and, in fact, looked alarmingly fit and raring to go. We decided to keep him for a couple of days and then release him on one of the large commons on the outskirts of London where foxes were frequently seen.

By the following morning, there was complete chaos in the garage. What the fox had not broken or dismantled he had chewed or eaten. He sat on his throne of boxes again, grinning at me as I peeked through my crack in the door. He was in charge and letting me know it.

We only had a few casualties at that time but a couple of them were quite bizarre and, although rescued, really had no place in the British countryside so I had to find them a suitable home. The first was a fully grown Florida terrapin that was found abandoned, presumably after it had outgrown the tiny fish tank it was sold in. The other was an enormous Indian python that I was convinced would have eaten all of us, given the chance. I had arranged a home for these two at a marine centre in London, so I planned to take the fox along and release him on the way.

With Sue, Colin and Julie the dog all in the car, and the animals packed in cardboard carrying cases, we set off for the metropolis. This was a mistake! I now know that foxes eat cardboard and before we had travelled far along the M40, a glimpse in my rear-view mirror showed 'King fox' sitting up and grinning back at me. His box was in tatters and he had also managed to release the other two in a pandemonium of snake, terrapin and fox, all in the back of my small estate car.

I pulled over on the hard shoulder to formulate a battle plan. I could not open the back of the car, or King fox would be straight out into the middle of the motorway.

The release of our first fox

There was no other solution but for Sue to clutch hold of Colin and Julie onto her lap, while I clambered over the seats to make a grab for the fox.

Thinking coldly and calculatingly, I got Sue to give me Julie's collar and lead. I managed to get the collar onto the fox and anchor the lead firmly to my very heavy toolbox in the back of the car, all without getting bitten. The terrapin was not a threat and I could construct one good box out of the three the fox had ripped up to house the snake, and so continue our journey to freedom.

You have never heard such a sigh of relief as when our three passengers had gone to their respective destinies in London and we had an empty, albeit a bit smelly, car in which to visit my parents in South London for a reviving cup of tea.

Now, after I have rescued, handled, treated and released hundreds of foxes, I can look back and smile at those early days and the panic that each new fox instilled in us. We made mistake after mistake but gradually learned the ups and downs of fox care. Most of the mistakes only cost us time and anguish, like the three nights we both sat outside the pen of fox cubs to keep them quiet and stop them disturbing the neighbours with the caterwauling play that can destroy a housing estate in the middle of the night.

Sue with Blossom, our first cub

The foxes, with one tragic exception, never suffered from our mistakes, I hope. That exception taught me a sad lesson I will remember for the rest of my life: *never, ever to keep foxes in the house.*

Blossom was our first fox cub. She was so small and dark brown that we were not quite sure whether she was a fox or some type of dog. Sue spent many hours feeding the little mite, even bringing her into the bedroom at night so that she could answer each little whimper with a bottle of warm milk substitute designed for puppies.

Poppet, our little spaniel who had replaced Julie when she died, loved Blossom and would gloat over her as though she was her own puppy. This was our first big mistake, but it's so easy to see with hindsight how wrong we were to allow a fox, a wild animal, to become friends with a dog, which is probably the only enemy, apart from man, that British foxes have to be wary of. We just didn't think; or did we, deep down, hope that Blossom could join us as a family pet? Another misjudgement.

Blossom with Poppet, our Cavalier spaniel who treated her like her own puppy

Blossom grew and grew, her bright blue eyes opened and she got her first little teeth. She began to look like a fox but by then we had made another mistake: she was far too friendly. As soon as she spotted one of us, back would go her ears, her tiny tail would windmill round and round and her little pants of joy told us she loved to be loved.

Very quickly she outgrew the large, wire cage in which she slept, although she was often allowed to run around the living room. Our dossier of mistakes mounted. To give her more room I combined two playpens which had bars close enough together to contain her, or so I thought.

She did not like being confined and I was already seeing how wrong we were not to keep her at arm's length and wild, but she still panted at our approach with little squeaks of excitement. She seemed happy; but finally all my mistakes culminated in disaster.

One day, as I hurried down our dark staircase to meet the postman, I trod on something soft but unseen. It was Blossom. She had somehow got out of her pen and climbed upstairs to greet me. I had not seen her sitting on the stair and I fell from top to bottom with her beneath me. At the bottom she lay gasping, blood pouring from her mouth. I didn't know what to do, but gathered her up quickly and drove like a lunatic to the vet's. Richard Hill, a

I want to give every injured fox a chance to live

really dedicated vet, dropped everything and tried all he knew to save her, but to no avail. I had killed this wonderful little animal by my own selfishness and stupidity. We had had no right to bring her into the house and to this day no other wild animal has ever been allowed inside. I had a broken arm to remind me of the accident, though I needed no reminder: even now I can see that beautiful little fox and the horrific accident that ended her life.

I learned a lot that day and have since met hundreds of foxes and fox cubs. Every one is different; every one has in its eyes some untold story, and a will to live which is second to none. I give them all, injured, sick or orphaned, a chance of life and will do all in my power to defend their right to live. The trouble is that the fox's reputation has always been tainted by the stories told against it, but once you get to know a fox and understand its charisma, you will find that we have the supreme wild animal right on our own doorstep and we should cherish each moment we spend in its company.

CHAPTER ONE

THE MUD STICKS

Samson foxes

Most wild animal casualties which arrive at a rescue
centre are in a state of severe shock. This is not the shock
we feel when someone 'makes us jump', but a collapse of
the body's circulatory system in a downward spiral which
quickly results in death. At the Wildlife Hospital Trust we
have a tried and tested 'crash' treatment of intravenous
drugs and fluids that can reverse the shock and save an
animal's life.

It is a technical, complicated procedure, one of the first
steps of which is to shave an area on one of the animal's
front legs with specially designed electric clippers. It takes
only one stroke to clip badgers and deer but as you try to
shave a fox's leg, you soon realise that underneath that
majestic red coat there is another coat of tightly curled
hair that resists even the most immaculate clippers. The
density of this extra woolly coat is such that foxes are said
not to feel the cold until the temperature reaches minus
15 degrees Centigrade – almost equivalent to the temperature of one of our household deep-freeze cabinets.

It is this woolly coat that inspired one of the most lasting references to foxes. It originated in the Old Testament and is still in use today. Field naturalists and wildlife rescue centres occasionally meet foxes which have only a close, woolly undercoat. These are known as Samson foxes, for the Old Testament figure, renowned for his own hair loss, is reputed to have tied burning brands to the tails of 300 foxes, sending them to fire the Philistines' crops. The foxes' main fur would have been singed away, but the woolly undercoat would have resisted for a while, giving the animals the appearance of unclipped poodles.

In fact even the human condition 'alopecia', or hair loss, derives its name from *alopex*, the Greek word for fox.

Fox fables

Though not many of us will find ourselves discussing a Samson fox over a cup of coffee, the phrase 'It's only sour grapes' still crops up regularly in conversation. It dates back to about 600 BC to a fable by Aesop, that remarkable slave, who told stories to free himself from the shackles of bondage. Aesop always disguised a message in his stories and in this particular fable the fox's very human behaviour illustrates that people often pretend to dislike things they are unable to get.

> A hungry fox went into a vineyard where there were fine ripe grapes. Unfortunately for him, the grapes were growing on a trellis so high up that he was not able to reach them. 'Oh well, never mind!' said the fox. 'Anyone can have them for all I care. They are sure to be sour.'

This idea that foxes have a penchant for grapes appears elsewhere in literature. Was it a myth, I wondered, or based on sound observation?

At the time of writing I had several foxes in the Wildlife

Hospital and, knowing that they will eat almost anything, I bought a few different types of grape and put the myth to the test. Most of the foxes proved too wild to betray their likes or dislikes but Bob, a fox injured on a local RAF base and quite used to being given titbits by the airmen and their families, drooled at every grape, proving them to be a great new stimulant to make him exercise a weakened ankle damaged in his accident.

Aesop was right, but whether his fables were the result of direct observation is not clear. Certainly, his satires became the popular reference for many other writers, with the fondness for grapes constantly turning up, even in the *Song of Solomon*: 'Take us the foxes, the little foxes that spoil the vines: for our vines have tender grapes.'

Unlike the Reynard the Fox stories which were popular in the Middle Ages, Aesop's stories were intended for children and carried messages of value to young minds, with the fox illustrating the pitfalls of flattery ('The Fox and the Crow' and 'The Fox and the Hen'), familiarity ('The Fox and the Lion') and idle chatter ('The Fox and the Wolf'). There were also some whose messages were more subtle, like 'The Fox and the Cock', in which punishment overtakes the evildoer.

One very interesting fable that many people today would do well to heed is 'The Fox and the Hedgehog'. Using horseflies as the analogy, the fox rejects the hedgehog's offer to rid him of pestering flies, commenting that if you destroy one pest the vacuum left will soon be filled by another, who may be more of a nuisance than the original pest. I think that in modern Britain farmers regret killing foxes, as they are now being pestered by an upsurge of rats, mice and rabbits – Aesop's prediction going unheeded.

Fact and fancy

In the main, Aesop's fables have been remembered through the centuries. Similarly, his fellow countryman Aristotle, who lived 200 years later, is remembered for his factual commentaries. In his *Historia Animalium*, he got his one reference to the fox all wrong by stating that cubs 'were born unarticulated and had to be licked into shape by the vixen', an observation finally refuted by Pierandrea Mattioli in the sixteenth century. The phrase 'licked into shape', though, still features in popular conversation, even if the 'unarticulation' has long since been forgotten.

After Aristotle, natural history writing becomes a bit fanciful, led by Aelian in the second century before Christ, who told of how foxes trapped wasps in their tails so that they could rob the wasps' nests, and used their silhouettes to attract and catch bustards. These obvious inventions were generally ignored by later writers, but Aelian's stories of foxes catching fish with their tails or urinating on hedgehogs to make them unroll prospered, with Olaus Magnus using the fishing myth in his illustration of AD 1555. Some people today still believe and repeat the hedgehog yarn.

Gaius Plinius Secondus (Pliny), the prolific Roman soldier-scholar who died in the eruption at Pompeii in AD 79, hardly mentions the fox in his mammoth *Natural History*, which was largely based on some of his own observations and the writings of others, including Aristotle. Sadly, his one reference to the fox seems to be a complete fabrication. It describes how the fox forms a partnership with ravens to fight a common enemy, a small bird called an aesolon that was said to prey on ravens' eggs.

Another Greek, Plutarch, was writing at about this time

and maintained: 'A fox is not caught twice in the same snare.' I don't think his statement has lasted but horrifically the use of snares to catch foxes has. It is still legal in Britain, a touch of barbarism maintained from the age of throwing Christians to the lions.

If a fox should survive its first encounter with a snare, which is most unlikely, unless it is rescued and treated for the inevitable injury, it will quickly revert to its established paths and will be garrotted again. At the Hospital we regularly see this flaw in foxes' intelligence when we have to handle them with a piece of equipment called a 'grasper'. In handling foxes and badgers, the grasper – a thick, plastic-covered noose at the end of a pole – is slid over the animal's head to bring the creature under control, reducing the chance of one of us getting badly bitten. The noose does the animal no harm as it is a lot thicker than a snare and has, at times, actually enabled us to save many lives. The badger, which is generally accepted as having far less intelligence than the fox, uses the first encounter to learn how to avoid the grasper: it tucks its head between its front legs. The fox, however, appears totally naïve, keeps its head up and is simply caught in the noose again, not merely a second time, but as many times as we need to handle it for treatment. So, in spite of what Plutarch and the gamekeepers may say, a snare is always lethal, even to a fox who survives the first strangulation.

Vulpis the fox from a twelfth-century bestiary

The fox as villain

The fox may be susceptible to the subterfuge of the game-keeper but generally it is master of its own environment; a creature of the dark and the shadows that moves with stealth and purpose, an SAS soldier of the animal kingdom. This lifestyle makes the fox a very difficult animal to study, even with today's sophisticated optical accoutrements, so imagine the quandary of the early zoologists, who did not have the benefit of binoculars, night sights and thermal underwear for clear, frosty, night vigils. Consequently, when the first major natural history work since Pliny's was written, in the fifth century AD, probably by an anonymous Greek monk, its contents were fiction, based largely on the personifications of Aesop's fables, rather than fact. However, this *Physiologus* or *Natural History*, became the foundation for the famous bestiaries of the Middle Ages; although it had been suppressed for decades as heretical, its contents resurfaced in the twelfth century in a famous bestiary now housed in a library at Cambridge and translated by T. H. White in 1954. Here we are given the baffling information that *vulpes*, the Latin name for the fox is derived from *volupis*, a person who winds wool. According to the origination the fox is 'a creature with circuitous pug marks who never runs straight but goes on his way with tortuous windings.' Those who have seen the rigid straight lines of a fox's track across snow-covered ground would probably disagree, but the slight misrepresentation has done foxes no harm. Far more damaging is the rest of this section of the bestiary, which goes on to describe the fox as 'a fraudulent and ingenious animal with the Devil's nature of feigning death until the birds (people's souls) approach close enough to be caught'.

This, of course, did nothing for the fox's reputation among an uneducated and God-fearing populace and, coupled with the Reynard the Fox sagas of the time, the publication blackened the fox's character for many hundreds of years, and is still believed by many people in Europe and Asia.

Other bestiaries appeared, compounding the diabolical felony of playing dead. Olaus Magnus added to this, and to the tail-fishing myth, yet another spurious exploit – that the fox can divest itself of fleas. It is supposed to take a clump of grass in its mouth and gradually back into a pool or stream until only its snout and the grass remain above the surface. To avoid drowning, the fleas, or lice (as E. T. Seton suggested as recently as 1929), jump into the clump of grass, which the fox then releases. This is nonsense. It is all the more ludicrous because foxes never have many fleas, and in the hundreds of foxes that I have handled, I have never once seen one troubled with lice. Perhaps Magnus's claim, made in the sixteenth century, was the precursor of the 'foxes are dirty' stigma that still plagues the fox today, even though we are constantly showing that foxes are among the cleanest animals in the countryside.

Misinformation about the fox in a drawing by Olaus Magnus (1555)

The odds were gradually stacking against the fox and when the apothecaries started prescribing parts of foxes for curing various ills, it seemed that everybody was out to kill the maligned animals. It must have been a gruesome business to be sick in the Middle Ages and it was particularly bad news for foxes: their blood was used to promote hair growth; their private parts, slung around the neck, eased headaches and teething; any fat relieved gout and cramped muscles, and a brain rendered children safe from epilepsy. The most repulsive 'remedy' of all, however, was a fox's tongue worn as a brooch to prevent blindness.

I had hoped that Gestner's work, also produced in the sixteenth century, might absolve the fox and relieve the persecution, but Topsell's translation of 1607 showed the work to be as much a mixture of fact and fiction as its fore-runners, with an added physiological gem: the information that a fox's legs are shorter on one side and so it can run only one way around a hill.

This fanciful suggestion has apparently faded into antiquity but some of the fox exploits described in this chapter seem to have endured, even up to the present day, especially the fleas in the water trick reiterated by Tommy Trips in 1767, by Ernest Thompson Seton in 1929, and in countless other manuals of natural history.

During the Middle Ages, however, most natural history commentators preferred describing fabulous beasts like unicorns, dragons, or amphisbenas with two heads, rather than foxes. It was the satirists who, from the seventh century onwards, perpetuated the parables of Reynard the Fox, casting the animal as an artful knave, a safe way of highlighting the evils of rulers and priests at a period when it was considered foolhardy even to think about criticising one's betters.

The fox did not stand a chance; in every story, from Redegar's Chronicle of AD 612 onwards, Reynard was portrayed as treacherous, devious and callous (in fact he was

Reynard being hanged by the geese while the watch-dogs bark triumphantly (St Michael's Church, Brent Knoll, Somerset

given every trait that people would find abhorrent in a man). All over Europe, year after year, the character assassination gathered momentum. In the ninth and tenth centuries numerous Latin poems circulated the charges, and in 1148 Nivardus of Ghent revived the image of 'Reinardus Vulpes'.

The Church joined the campaign with many carvings illustrating the crimes of the evil Reynard. Those on the misericords in Bristol Cathedral are especially striking; they illustrate the villain's treacherous behaviour to Tibert the cat and Bruin the bear, and even to the King's messengers, eventually culminating in the scoundrel's trial and execution – a scene depicted in many churches all over the country. A well-known preacher, Odo of Cheriton, even used parables about Reynard in his sermons, adding to the contempt his congregations were already feeling towards their neighbours, the foxes.

And it gets worse: another major version, *Reinaed de Vos*, hit the bookstalls in 1250, reinforced in the late fourteenth century by Geoffrey Chaucer in his *Canterbury Tales* where, in 'The Nonne's Preeste's Tale', the fox, called Russel, abducts everybody's hero, Chanticleer the

cockerel, only to be finally beaten by the cock's flattery –
again a major human failing.

By this time most people believed the adage that foxes
are verminous and the torrent continued, an anonymous
author of 1370 expanding the legend with another 4,000
lines. And William Caxton printed an English version in
1481, making it available to even more readers.

William Shakespeare, thankfully, brought a modicum of
sanity with over thirty references to the guile and intelligence of foxes gleaned from his own observations rather
than from the myriad of sensational tales written before
his time. But another Elizabethan dramatist, John Lyly,
declared: 'When the fox preacheth, the geese perish.' Poor
old fox had now become a treacherous preacher – a new
twist. Just how low could a fox get?

A timely respite followed, but soon the antagonists were
back, with an eighteenth-century writer, Lessing, claiming
in his fables that the fox was 'a rogue wishing to appear
honest'. Another writer, Thomas Fuller, had picked up the
religious theme: 'It's a silly goose that comes to the fox's
sermon.'

In 1826 the Reynard stories grew by 40,000 lines when
Roman du Renard was published in Paris by Meon. Despite
the fact that Reynard the anti-hero ended up on the gallows, the writers were not outdone; they came up with a
solution: *Son of Reynard!* In this tale the unfortunate fox's
progeny, Reynardine, was as treacherous as his father, but
with more religious overtones: he adopted a monk's cloth-
ing to deceive his goose victims. His deceptions are
reflected for ever in a stained glass window of St Martin's
Church, Leicester, which bears the inscription '*Testis est
mihi Deus quam cupiam vos visceribus meis*', which when

translated means: 'God is my witness how much I long for you in my bowels'.

Most of us know nothing of the Reynard stories, but looking through them it is easy to see that phrases from them are still current in everyday life. How many of today's unfortunate tame bears are known as 'Bruin'? And how many times have you called someone a 'silly goose'?

Today's enemies of the fox have been manipulated into that position over the centuries. Much of the propaganda which shapes their opinions originated in the Dark Ages. The constant abuse hurled at the fox has dragged the reputation of this most splendid animal down to the level where many people consider it to be vermin – a term I despise but which literally means noxious, troublesome, or objectionable animals, and which is popularly applied to foxes, rats and mice, believed to be harbingers of dirt and disease.

The fox as hero

But all was not lost. Almost imperceptibly, some good comments were starting to creep into popular literature. The brothers Grimm were in the vanguard of the trend and although their fairy-tales do include stories of fox treachery, especially in 'The Godmother Wolf', as the wolf had always received a worse press than the fox, this time the fox was almost a hero. The Grimms showed the Fox being helpful to the Horse, with no repercussions; a bit gullible faced with the Cat; and totally naïve when he was outwitted by his old adversaries, the Geese. Perhaps the better press occurred because the brothers Grimm appear to have overlooked the bestiaries and the Reynard stories and to have based their tales on those of Aesop and

Cubs as they really are

his predecessors, especially in their story 'The Fox and the Cat', which carries the message that 'the fox had hundreds of tricks but the cat only one', a statement reminiscent of the poet Archilochus who wrote in 700 BC that 'the fox has hundreds of tricks but the hedgehog only one'.

At last with the dawn of the twentieth century the fictional fox lost some of his deviousness and became, if you like, possessed of human frailty. Beatrix Potter's Mr Tod was both gullible and, for a change, unimportant, with the rabbits getting the upper hand just as Brer Rabbit did in the contemporary tales of Uncle Remus. Although in that Brer Fox story the fox tried the timeless 'playing dead' trick featured in the old manuscripts, he was outwitted by the dominant rabbit.

Gradually the fox, despised for centuries, was getting a better reception. At last we were seeing images of a wild animal without all the despicable human traits of deceit and treachery. Calling Field Marshal Rommel the 'Desert Fox' during the Second World War in North Africa carried a degree of respect for a master tactician, despite the

Foxes on postage stamps: a source of national pride

fact that he was an enemy to those who coined this name for him.

The world took many years to recover from that 1939–45 war, but by 1960 a new, less formal outlook on life seemed to blossom with new images and, most important of all, new thinking. Television had arrived and assailed us with programmes like *Look* and *Zoo Quest*, giving most of us our first glimpses of the incredible real-life world of the wild animal, the world of the fox. All of a sudden there were no foxes slaughtering chickens, but good, caring parents mothering adorable little cubs and killing only because they had to feed their family and themselves, in that order. At last we saw foxes as they really are: at the top of that food chain the conservationists are always telling us about. Up there to be respected and protected along with other countries' lions, tigers and killer whales.

There were more magazines and books available glorifying images of handsome foxes, along with those lions and tigers. Then suddenly letters emerging from the hardpressed bleak oppressed countries of the Eastern Bloc

The only fox to be seen in parts of the countryside

landed on our door mats with postage stamps celebrating their own wildlife. Countries like Poland, Hungary, Albania, East Germany and Yugoslavia showed us that their foxes were the same as ours, but were apparently appreciated as an asset, not labelled as vermin. Even though some countries, like Russia, highlighted foxes' value as fur-bearers, most countries showed them as foxes in their natural surroundings – all except a series of stamps from France that included one of *Le Renard* in an urban setting with what could be construed as a gallows in the background. The ancient Reynard the Fox stories were always more popular in France. I only hope we are not due for another reprint.

All around the world countries followed the eastern European lead. Switzerland, Sweden, Romania, Burundi, Korea, Botswana and many others showed us their foxes – although some of them have succumbed to the old persecution and have become endangered, with a fear of extinction hanging over them.

But where are the British foxes? Presumably they were still carrying out the dastardly deeds of folklore, for even though they are at the pinnacle of what's left of our wildlife heritage, only recently have they squeezed onto Royal Mail packets, not as wild animals to be proud of, but as symbols of wintertime – their world, where they leave us puny humans shivering in their wake.

Slowly, I think, we are changing our attitudes to the fox. Although Oscar Wilde's 'unspeakables' in their pursuit of the 'uneatable' still slander the fox and accuse him of committing all manner of preposterous misdemeanours, the younger generation give us hope. The foxes they know and warm to are Foxy Loxy or Basil Brush cracking 'Boom, Boom' jokes on television. They like the fox and, thanks to Roald Dahl's *Fantastic Mr Fox*, who saved all the woodland animals from the gluttonous farmers, think of him as a hero. The epitome of the 'good guy', the fox was shown by Walt Disney in the role of Robin Hood, with Maid Marian beside him, robbing the rich to feed the poor. And in 1992 Tails the Fox was partnered with Sonic the Hedgehog as everybody's heroes in the biggest-selling computer game of all time. Who could possibly hate foxes after those commendations.

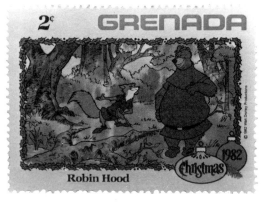

A Disney hero: the fox as Robin Hood

CHAPTER TWO

FOXES AROUND THEIR WORLD

Fox species

While most natural history writing had, through the ages, included some fact among an awful lot of fiction, it failed to tell anybody about the different species of fox striving for survival around the world. Obviously most commentaries arising in Europe and the British Isles discussed the familiar red fox, but what about the 'little foxes' mentioned in the *Song of Solomon*? Were these the enchanting fennec foxes, the smallest known, or even Rüppell's sand foxes (which look like small, pale red foxes with larger ears)? There was probably only one species of fox, the red, present in civilised Europe during historic times but even in Britain, in prehistoric times before written records, there were Arctic foxes living at the edges of the glaciers before the recession of the last Ice Age, about ten thousand years ago.

Whatever the species of fox, or wherever it comes from, foxes are all members of the dog family, the *Canidae*, and are carnivorous. This indicates that all except one – the bat-eared fox – possess shearing carnassial teeth (the last upper premolar and first lower molar), which have sharp

A red fox at night, master of the dark

tips and jagged edges and are used for tearing flesh, the main food item of most carnivores. The *Canidae* have further evolutionary modifications to suit their lifestyle including the fusion of wrist bones and long bones in the front legs that enables them swiftly to pursue prey over the grassland, desert, or tundra where most foxes are to be found.

Foxes are the largest sub-family of the *Canidae* with fourteen recognised species, or twenty-one if we count in the seven South American 'almost' foxes. They may have suffered at the hands of the smear-mongers but their larger cousins, the wolves, coyotes and jackals, still carry a far greater social stigma, matched by no other species except perhaps the rat. Other members of the family are probably not as well known and include dholes, raccoon dogs, bush dogs, dingoes and African wild dogs, as well as the domestic dog.

Over the centuries foxes have not been domesticated but some neolithic remains of about 4500 BC suggest that in some areas they were kept either for food or as fur-bearers. Foxes do not make good pets – these days many wildlife rescue centres run campaigns to deter people from taming them – and, once tamed, cannot be rehabilitated to the wild.

Evolution

The ancestors of all the carnivorous species known today – dogs, cats, mustelids, civets, mongooses, hyenas – evolved in the Eocene period, some 40 million years ago, from the Miacoidea, a group of primitive forest-dwelling animals. Two separate paths of evolution lead down from the Miacoidea, foxes and jackals developing from the Cynodictis, and dogs and wolves from the Amphicyon. This happened in the Oligocene period, at least 26 million years ago or perhaps as much as 38 million years. All the ancestral species have long since become extinct. Many of the dog species died out during the ensuing Miocene period so that in today's Pleistocene period we are left with only ten sub-families (genera) of the *Canidae* family.

Fossil records of individual species are at best sparse and their interpretation is constantly open to debate. Our native fox, the red fox, has been traced to a direct ancestor, the *Vulpes alopecoides*, which lived between 600,000 and 400,000 years ago. The red fox itself, *Vulpes vulpes*, first crops up in fossil records from the middle Pleistocene period, about 400,000 years ago.

In more modern times, at the time of the last glaciation, there were three species of evolved fox thriving in Europe; but as the ice sheet receded the Arctic fox followed it to the far north while the corsac fox retreated to the steppes of Russia, leaving just the red fox resident over the rest of the continent. All around the world the different fox species were settling into their niches, and these have not changed since, except where man's interference has either introduced foxes to new habitats or else destroyed whole territories with trapping and agriculture. However, there are still fourteen species of fox across the world, and there are some 'foxes' that are not really foxes at all, some that are not even related to foxes and others that are still the subject of argument between taxonomists, the people who classify different fauna into genera and species.

Foxes in name only

First, let us look at those animals which are mistakenly thought of as foxes, before we investigate the true fox.

It's not the taxonomists who have a problem with the **flying fox**. This animal's popular name was probably given to it as a result of its having a furry face and neck, with bright eyes, but those who named it seem to have overlooked its large membranous wings and the fact that it spends the day hanging upside-down in trees. The flying fox is actually a bat – a fruit bat, to be more precise – and is not even remotely related to the true foxes.

Living in a different element, the **fox shark** is obviously not a fox nor does it prey on foxes. But what about the Simien fox, portrayed on the stamps of Ethiopia? Or the peculiarly named vinegar fox of the Amazon basin? Are these foxes or just other popular misnomers?

They are both members of the dog family, the *Canidae*, but the **Simien fox** seems to confound everybody. At the moment taxonomists agree on it as the Simien jackal, *Canis simensis*, but also that it was once the Simien fox. It has at times been called the Abyssinian wolf as well as the Ethiopian jackal. But the **vinegar fox** has, to my knowledge, only ever had this one nickname. In reality it is the bush dog, *Speothos venaticus*, with short legs and ears, bearing no resemblance whatsoever to a fox. And, come to think of it, bearing very little resemblance to a dog.

Another South American Canid, the maned wolf *Chrysocyon brachyurus*, has often been called the **fox-on-stilts**. True, it does not look much like a wolf, but then its weight at twenty-three kilograms would make it a really enormous fox. Actually the taxonomists have classified it as neither and have given it a genus all of its own: another fox that is not a fox.

The 'almost' foxes

South America, does, however, have its own range of foxes, the *Dusicyon*, but as they are classified midway between the true foxes, *Vulpes*, and the dogs and wolves, *Canis*, I would like to treat them as 'almost' foxes and provide just a minimum of information to distinguish them from the vulpine and other foxes that are the main subject of this chapter.

Basically they have typically fox-like habits with a similar dietary pattern of being able to subsist on a mixture of vegetable matter, insects and carrion if fresh meat is not obtainable. In addition the crab-eating fox will, whenever possible, top up its table with crustaceans.

There are seven recognised species of these South American 'almost' foxes, split into two groups: the culpeo (one species) and the romantically named zorros (six species), which take their name from the Spanish word for foxes.

The culpeo, *Dusicyon culpaeus*, is known as the South American red fox or the **culpeo fox**. It is often larger than our native red fox and can be found in Argentina, Peru, Chile and Bolivia. The zorros are smaller than the culpeo and feature in most other South American countries where, in many cases, they are under pressure – as are so many animals of that continent, both from persecution and loss of habitat.

The largest of the zorros is the **small-eared zorro**, *Dusicyon microtis*, weighing in at nine to ten kilograms and still larger than our familiar red fox. It is hardly ever seen, probably for its own good, resulting in very little information being available on the present status of its population.

Much smaller and better known, the **crab-eating zorro**, *Credocyn thous*, also known as the crab-eating fox, the common fox and even the forest fox, is not so fortunate and is killed for its low-value pelt in most of the north-eastern countries of South America where it is generally distributed and fairly common.

The **grey zorro**, *Dusicyon griseus*, is the South American grey fox found in Chile and Argentina. It suffers major losses to the fur trade, though it does have some degree of government protection – apparently not always effective. It has also suffered as the much larger culpeo expands into its range.

It does not pay to be well known if you are a zorro. The other familiar zorro, *Dusicyon gymnocercus*, known as **Azara's zorro** and Azara's fox, also enjoys some legal protection, but, each year, many thousands of pelts are illegally shipped from Brazil, Uruguay, Paraguay and Argentina.

The other two zorro species may be escaping persecution due to their elusive habits, but nobody really knows the present status of the **small hoary zorro**, *Dusicyon vetulus*, also known as the hoary fox or small-toothed dog, which may be suffering from changing agricultural practices and deforestation, or of the remaining South American fox, the **Sechuran zorro**, *Dusicyon sechurae*, from the borders of Peru and Ecuador, about which there is hardly any information whatsoever, except that its tail and body length is 78–84cm and its weight is 4–5 kilograms.

The true foxes

All the other foxes, the true members of the fox family around the world, belong to one of three genera: the twelve vulpine foxes, *Vulpes*, including the fennec fox and the grey fox (recently given their own separate classification); the Arctic fox, *Alopex*; and the bat-eared fox, *Otocyon*.

The **bat-eared fox**, *Otocyon megalotisis*, is unlike its relatives in that is has largely forsaken mammalian prey for a diet of insects, in particular the termite *Hodotermes mossambicus*. It will, like other foxes, eat fruit and some vegetable matter and has been seen matching its dexterity at hunting against the gerbil's quicksilver reactions around the latter's colonies. However, a glance at the bat-eared fox's teeth will immediately show how through evolution it has adapted to its mainly insectivorous diet; in fact, they are reminiscent of a large mole's or shrew's, with needle-sharp canines backed with rows of small sharp-pointed, similar-sized teeth that are ideal for cracking the hard chitinous skins of insects. Gone are the meat-shearing carnassial teeth of the carnivore. Counting the teeth also brings a surprise in that this fox has developed an extra tooth on each side of its jaw, giving it more teeth than any other placental mammal (but not marsupials), except for the toothed whales and dolphins.

The bat-eared fox inhabits the open grassland and semi-desert of Southern and Central Africa, notably southern Zambia, Angola and South Africa. It also lives further north in a band from the Sudan down the east coast to Tanzania. As recently as during the last twenty-five years it has moved into parts of Mozambique, Zimbabwe and Botswana, probably by following colonies of its preferred prey: the termite.

As well as developing tiny insectivorous teeth, the bat-eared fox has also evolved over-size ears to help it

Bat-eared fox, Otocyon megalotisis

cope with the hot arid climate of its homeland. Although not as large as those of its North African cousin, the fennec fox, its ears, tipped with black, are up to twelve centi-metres long. They help to dispel excess body heat while at the same time collecting the small intri-cate sounds of its bland environment. Most of its search-ing for prey occurs at night but it occasionally forages during the day if not lying up in long grass or under rocks or bushes, taking part in communal grooming.

The bat-eared fox is quite a bit smaller than our familiar red fox but is also, surprisingly, considerably larger than many of the other species. It weighs up to four and a half kilograms, a lot bigger than most genuine insectivores which tend to be smaller to compensate for their minuscule prey. It grows to about sixty-six centimetres long with an extra thirty centimetres of bushy fox tail. The overall colour is a greyish-buff with a paler underside and a black stripe along its back that handsomely complements its black front legs and the black markings on its face, tail and hind legs.

This fox's way of life seems to be geared to termite colonies. Unusually for foxes, unrelated animals will be seen together at the colonies, taking advantage of the harvest that the rainy season brings. The breeding season varies from country to country, occurring in the wake of the rains to benefit from the flush of termites triggered by the downpours.

If you are surprised at the size of the bat-eared fox's ears then you will be amazed at those of another African fox, the tiny *Fennecus zerda* of Morocco, Algeria, Tunisia, Libya, Egypt and some of the

Fennec fox, Fennecus zerda

Sudan and Sinai. This, the **fennec fox**, is arguably the prettiest of the foxes but is definitely the smallest, with a body length of only about thirty-five centimetres, the size of a chihuahua. Its very long bushy tail is nearly as long again and its body is topped with the most wonderful ears, fifteen centimetres long – almost half the length of its body. Foxes are unable to perspire excess body temperature so these enormous ears act like a car radiator, dispersing the heat which accumulates in the fennec's desert home.

Perfectly adapted for a life in the hot dry deserts of

North Africa, the fennec, which weighs no more than one and a half kilograms, also keeps itself cool by lying during the day in deep burrows up to ten metres underground where the sand insulates it against the high surface temperatures. Fennecs excavate their own burrows and it is said that a fennec can dig its way out of sight in an instant.

They will only venture out of these burrows in the cool of the night when they will hunt for scorpions, insects, reptiles, the occasional small mammal and various plant foods. This diet provides all the fennec's moisture requirements so it has no need to drink – although it will if water is available.

Being so small they are in constant danger from hyenas, jackals, vultures and even Bedouin Arabs who trap and hunt them as pets and even as food. However, possessing the super-sensitivities of a fox the fennec is pretty good at evading capture, especially by humans. The Arabs know its capabilities only too well:

Two dogs make a fennec play
Three make him laugh
Four make him run about
Five make him flee, and
Six dogs finally catch him.

Not bad for such a tiny animal, but perhaps no surprise knowing the mental and physical resources of the whole fox family.

The Americans have their own version of a long-eared fox which lives in the deserts and grasslands of the western United States. This is the **kit fox**, *Vulpes velox*, now native to Montana, Dakota, Wyoming, Colorado, Nebraska, Kansas, Oklahoma and north-west Texas. At one time its range spread right across the grasslands of the United

States and into Canada, hence its other popular name 'prairie fox'. Attempts are being made to reintroduce the kit fox to Canada for conservation reasons, a far cry from the olden days when foxes were introduced purely for hunting, and a welcome change.

Once again the taxonomists are in a dither and cannot decide whether the kit fox is a different species from the **swift fox**. And as there are many accepted sub-species, only a scientist could highlight any difference, and probably only then from the skeleton or from skull sizes – not much use to a live fox.

The kit fox at forty-nine centimetres long is slightly longer than the fennec and has an even finer tail of thirty centimetres. Its diet, like that of most foxes, consists of rabbits, hares, rodents, birds and insects. One particular family of two adults (they form a permanent pair bond) and their five cubs took to their nest burrow, over a period of eight

Swift fox, Vulpes velox

weeks, a total of thirty-two hares, two rabbits, ten rodents and eight birds. Not bad for such a small fox; and not a chicken or lamb in sight.

Kit foxes do get taken by the much larger coyotes, but as the latter are slaughtered by the use of 1,080 poisons, those foxes that escape poisoning themselves can prosper in the relatively predator-free environment.

Whereas the kit fox is prey to coyotes, its very close relative the **San Joaquin kit fox**, *Vulpes velox mutica*, is threatened by a far more sinister animal – the 'nodding donkeys' of America's oil wells in west central California. Now officially classed as threatened or endangered, the San Joaquin kit fox is the subject of numerous conservation research programmes sponsored by such various bodies as the National Guard, the US Department of Energy, the Nature Conservancy Council and the California Energy Commission.

California seems to attract not only film stars and oil magnates, but also small pockets of very rare foxes. Resident on just six islands, off the California coast, is another

Grey fox, Urocyon cinereoargenteus

small fox: the **island grey fox**, *Urocyon littoralis,* which scavenges the beaches, living on fruit and insects with the occasional small mammal, bird, reptile, or egg taken with typical fox opportunism. Making dens among the cacti did not keep it safe from the feral cats and dogs which swarmed over the islands, but now the island fox enjoys full legal protection and in true US movie tradition the navy has steamed to the rescue and cleared its predators, left over from man's habitation, away from some of the islands. As a further assurance of the species' survival the Los Angeles zoo has also established a captive breeding colony of this very rare little fox.

Across the rest of the United States the island fox's larger cousin, the **grey fox**, with its mouthful of a Latin name, *Urocyon cinereoargenteus,* lives in bushy woodland

and forested areas. Although it is quite a bit smaller than the red fox, the early European settlers still tried to hunt it on horseback with hounds. But the grey fox had a trick up its sleeve to thwart the 'halloa' brigade: it climbed trees. Not by clambering up a sloping trunk, as the red fox often does to escape being ripped asunder, but by genuinely climbing, with front legs clasped around a vertical trunk in a way reminiscent of a large squirrel. The grey fox is the only member of the *Canidae* to favour arboreal habits and will quite often den high up in hollow trees. It's probably not as dextrous as a squirrel once it is tree-borne but it can cope with very thin branches; a sad illustration of this occurred when an unfortunate grey fox caught its tail in the fork of two branches and died there; to have got into that position, it must have climbed branches no more than two centimetres thick.

The grey fox is trapped mercilessly for its fur but seems to be holding its own in the United States, and through Central America down as far as Venezuela. Once common in Canada, it was largely evicted when the hunting fraternity introduced European red foxes, but is now gradually making a comeback into its old haunts.

The **red fox**, *Vulpes vulpes*, has always been native to North America, but the population was far more scattered than today. It all stems from those early settlers who found very few red foxes to hunt and as the grey fox could thwart their bloodlust by climbing trees, they took it upon themselves to import umpteen European red foxes throughout the seventeenth and eighteenth centuries. In true hunting tradition, they no doubt protected their victims which soon settled down to breed with the native red foxes and rapidly colonised the whole of North America, from the

Arctic Circle to New Mexico.

The most wide-ranging and familiar of the foxes, *Vulpes vulpes*, is found right across most of Asia living at heights of 4,000 metres or more. It has colonised parts of North Africa and the whole of Europe including, of course, the British Isles, where it is absent only from the offshore islands of Scotland (though Skye does have a population of foxes which vie with a healthy population of otters as the prime mammalian predator).

In the nineteenth century huntsmen introduced foxes for sport to the marsupial world of Australia. At first it was only three animals in 1864, followed by several in 1870–71. Apparently, from this very meagre beginning the alien fox population exploded so much that, in 1929, a government-sponsored cull resulted in 893,000 foxes being slaughtered in Western Australia alone. Thank goodness the fox was not introduced to New Zealand along with the European hedgehog, *Erinaceus europaeus*, which thrives in the milder climate. Foxes would have had a field day at the expense of that country's indigenous populations of flightless birds and triggered off another fox cull programme of carnage.

The red fox populations occupy such a wide expanse of countries and habitats that there are bound to be size and colour differences between them and there may even be some which taxonomists might find important enough to classify as sub-species. But generally the red fox, weighing between five and ten kilograms, is considered to be just the right size for its lifestyle. Being neither too big nor too small the red fox manages to survive the most horrific persecution throughout its range but still it comes back for more, a credit to its stamina and adaptability.

For many cen-
turies, especially
when the much
larger wolves were
still present, the
fox was relatively
scarce in Britain
and could be vir-
tually ignored by
the thousands of
livestock farmers

Red fox, Vulpes vulpes

who at that time kept their poultry in open runs and ramshackle chicken coops. It was not until the hunting fraternity started importing Continental foxes to satisfy their
blood sport that there were anything like the number of
foxes we can see in the countryside these days. At one
time, in the nineteenth century, it was estimated that a
thousand foxes a year were sold through Leadenhall
Market alone and all were released into a landscape
devoid of any natural enemy.

It is said that the hill foxes found in Scotland and Ireland are larger than the rest of the native population
because their ancestry goes back to the more robust Scan-
dinavian foxes imported for 'better sport'. To give the English huntsmen a bit of the action too, some of these larger
animals were further translocated for hunts in the Mid-
lands and southern England.

It is generally believed by people with a concern for fox
welfare that hunting is just a form of inane cruelty that has
no effect on overall fox populations. The prime concern is
the carnage wreaked by vestiges of the gamekeeper profession who snare, trap, shoot and poison any animal or bird

that may threaten their pheasants or grouse. They kill or maim many thousands of animals and can have very deleterious effects on numbers, especially local populations, just like the fur trappers who use similar methods of slaughter to ply their evil trade.

There are still countless fox skins sold every year to succour the vanity of the few people who still have the insensitivity to wear furs. Their vanity has been responsible for the virtual extinction in Britain of the sought-after colour varieties of the red fox: the silver and the cross fox.

Most of us know the British red fox by its coat, sandy, red-brown or russet on top and pale underneath, complemented by black legs and ears and often, but not always, by a white tag to its tail. Some will have darker fur, some an almost black underneath, whereas the 'silver' fox, now virtually restricted to the far north of Europe, has a lustrous black coat with white tips to the long guard hairs giving it the handsome appearance that unfortunately makes it so popular in the fashion houses.

The poor old 'cross' fox also has the misfortune to be in demand for furs but, horrifically, the 'cross' (a black line down its back bisected by another across its shoulders) is visible only when the fox's skin is hung for tanning. Thank goodness the fur industry, at least in Britain, is in its death throes.

Whether it be for farming, sport, fur trading or rabies eradication programmes, the fox always needs to be on the run. But, as always, it seems aware of its predicament and is now turning to towns and cities to find sanctuary. The Bristol fox population has been seen by millions on various television programmes and now other foxes are following suit in cities like London, Stockholm, Montreal,

New York, Paris and many others all around the world. Foxes are perfectly at home in a park or in a garden and live happily on a diet of rats, mice, Chinese takeaways, bird-table offerings and bowls of dog food put out for hedgehogs. The only problems these urban foxes encounter are the inevitable motor cars and the misconception some householders have of their new neighbours.

Another fox that suffers chronic persecution, but which has no towns to turn to for comfort, is the diminutive **Arctic fox**, *Alopex lagopus*, of the cold and icy wastes of the frozen north. There may be no farms in their frozen hostile environment but still the trappers are there slaughtering the foxes for their fine winter coats. During the summer the Arctic foxes carry a grey-brown or chocolate-brown pelage but in the winter the white form, or morph, does actually go snow white, while the blue morph takes on a rich bluish-grey hue, both of which are much prized by furriers. So great is the demand for these fox furs that trappers will even brave the Arctic foxes' winter environment, where temperatures can drop as low as minus 40 degrees Centigrade. The foxes themselves have such good coats that apparently they do not even shiver at these low temperatures, and in one callous experiment were found to survive even at minus 73 degrees Centigrade, four times as cold as the household deep-freeze cabinet.

Of course, being a fox it is superbly adapted to suit its environment. The Arctic fox has short, thick legs and, in contrast to the large-eared foxes of the deserts, small stubby ears that restrict the loss of precious body heat. It even has hairs on the bottom of its feet, just like the largest of the land carnivores, the polar bear, which it follows over the pack ice to scavenge scraps from the giant predator's catches of seals and other prey.

In this hostile world of tundra and ice there is a distinct lack of sites suitable for dens, so the Arctic foxes use the same site over and over again for generation after generation and, rather like the badger sets in Britain, some have been continuously used for over 300 years.

The Arctic fox is found right across America, Greenland, Europe and Siberia at Arctic latitudes and has been spotted on pack ice hundreds of miles from shore. It does suffer dreadfully from human predation, with Iceland alone killing each year 45 per cent of its resident population and yet still, somehow, the little fox survives. But for how long? Some 37,000 Arctic fox skins were taken from North America, Greenland and Siberia in just the 1977–8 winter trapping season. No animal species can survive the loss of this many adults, even apart from the orgy of cruelty involved. Thankfully some countries like Norway, Sweden and Finland have introduced protective legislation, as have the greatest fur users of them all, the Russians, on Medniij Island, where the fox population was reduced to about a hundred survivors after a mange epidemic.

Arctic fox, Alopex lagopus

With protection the Arctic fox numbers will increase again to a self-balancing population in harmony with its environment. All foxes have a remarkable system of recovery, none more so than this little fox in its refrigerated homelands, but only legal protection and a ban on fur

Museum tableaux: the glow and grace of the living fox are missing

trading can ensure any future at all.

It is horrifying to me that trappers cannot see that, even though there appears to be a limitless supply of victims, their continued exploitation of any species can cause extinction. Unless measures are taken now, the Arctic fox and all its persecuted cousins in the dog family will exist only as ghastly, stiff, staring museum specimens.

One little-known fox that is slowly being hounded into oblivion is the **Bengal fox**, *Vulpes bengalensis*, a sandy orange fox with a black-tagged tail that used to inhabit the open, thorny-scrub countryside of the Indian sub-continent. On the plains of India this small fox has been largely exterminated for no reason whatsoever other than its pedigree as a fox. There is talk that it may survive on the newly created sanctuaries for bustards, but, as always, I am sceptical as I have seen how some bird conservationists view the fox that takes the occasional bird or its egg. There are still some scattered Bengal fox populations in Nepal and Pakistan so hopefully that mountainous terrain may see the fox through to a more enlightened world.

Nearby and reasonably safe higher up the Himalayan foothills, 5,000 metres above sea level, is the rarely seen **Tibetan sand fox**, *Vulpes ferrilata*. There are not many people at these high altitudes and apart from a few Tibetans who use fox skins for hats, there is no reason for it to be in conflict with man. Even the rodents, ground birds and lagomorphs that form its diet, especially the black-lipped pika, are remote from human habitation.

Just to the north-west of the Himalayan range is the home territory of one of the three original European foxes, the **corsac fox**, *Vulpes corsac*. Very little seems to be known about *V. corsac* other than that it is very similar to the red fox, has relatively longer legs and larger ears and, quite unfoxlike, hunts in small packs like dogs and wolves. It lives on the steppes and semi-desert of really remote areas like Transbaikalia, Turkestan, Mongolia, northern Manchuria, Afghanistan and south-eastern Russia. No wonder we do not know much about its lifestyle.

Spreading further westward into Iran, Saudi Arabia, Oman, Yemen, Jordan and Israel is a very tiny fox, **Blandford's fox**, *Vulpes cana*, also known as the hoary fox or Afghan fox. Being so small and subsisting on a frugivorous and insectivorous diet it cannot possibly be classed as a threat to man and his livestock. However, even though it is rare it is easy to trap and is consequently frequently taken for its skins. There is a locally abundant core of Blandford's foxes in Israel where it does enjoy protection and has a future.

Rüppell's fox, *Vulpes ruepelli*, occupies similar territory to Blandford's fox and even covers the North African territory of the fennec right across to Morocco. Hardly anything is known about this little fox other than that it seems to enjoy an omnivorous diet and could be gregarious in its habits. Any threat to it comes from predation by the much larger red fox and the indiscriminate use of poisons in Saudi Arabia.

Even less is known about the **pale fox**, *Vulpes pallida*, which is like a small red fox. It is found across the sandy and stony savanna of North Africa, across the Sahel from Senegambia to Kordofan, spreading through the semi-desert to the edge of the fennec territory. It seems to be mainly herbivorous and eats berries and fruits as well as the usual fox fare of meat and insects.

And finally there is the **Cape,** or **silver-backed fox,** *Vulpes chama*, of the far south of Africa. About half the size of a red fox, this grey or silver-grey fox has a reputation for taking livestock, though it's hard to imagine how such a small animal could be suspected. Consequently it is perse-cuted by South African farmers and by the Oranjejag, a registered hunting club of the Orange Free State, the gov-ernment of which pays 150 rand for each fox killed.

Its numbers are dwindling, and even though Cape Province has introduced protection for it at last, there is a loophole allowing the killing of problem wild animals. That, I am sure, gives farmers all the licence they need.

Though there are many species of fox, culpeo or zorro, all of them share a similar physiology differing only in size and colour (apart from the shapes of the ears, and the teeth of the bat-eared fox). This is the perfect physiology of a small carnivore adapted to a hunting existence in open country where the foxes can outwit or run down their prey and is surely the reason why they have managed to survive so long in a hostile world.

CHAPTER THREE

ABOUT THE FOX

Foxes' calls

Britain and the rest of the world may delight in a fair smattering of fox populations, but it is doubtful whether those people living right next door to a fox family will ever have the thrill of glimpsing their neighbours, even if the persecution abates and the numbers reach their natural balance. The adult fox is a master of the night and the shadows. It seldom lets itself be seen: hundreds of years of hounding have taught it to be wary and secretive. However, it displays no secrecy when it comes to vocalisation, particularly in the mating season. Many people have first learned of foxes in their neighbourhood when awoken by the unearthly banshee scream of a vixen. Renowned field naturalists and long-in-the-tooth countrymen have all been stopped in their tracks as a nearby vixen serenaded her partner.

The singing of a vixen, and her perfume, are pure seduction to a dog fox. He will answer with three or four staccato barks, sometimes followed by his version of the foxy scream. For decades scientists have tried to analyse and understand the calls of foxes, but all they have been able to tell us is that this vocabulary is made up of twenty-eight groups of sounds based on forty basic forms of sound production, an explanation as confusing as the fox calls themselves.

To my ears the calls of the foxes are the marriage vows of two animals totally devoted to each other. These conversations strengthen their relationship at the start of each mating season, cementing the 'pair bond', as naturalists would have it. And when one partner is lost or taken, its widow or widower keeps calling, but then the barks are lonely, despairing calls.

Orphaned and alone

I hear these calls all the time, as any fox patient brought to the Hospital is unavoidably separated from its spouse or its mother. A fox cub that has lost its mum will break your heart with its tiny, night-long, hopeless calls of an orphan. It is unavoidable: the animals in the hospital have to be there – for they could not survive outside until they are either fit again or grown to adulthood. Every night our corridors echo the sadness of being alone and there is no way I can assure those grieving foxes that it will be all right in the end. Happily, most adult foxes are with us for only a short time and are quickly returned to their own familiar territory.

Family groups

One of the worst repercussions of hunting, snaring, or shooting foxes, and one that is not publicised enough, is

A family of fox cubs

the destruction of the natural relationship between dog fox and vixen, or between both of them and their cubs. The fox is generally not promiscuous and lives its short life in a loose family group: a dog fox, a dominant vixen and several, often related, non-breeding vixens, which share a territory and the rearing of the dominant vixen's cubs. That is, until man intervenes and destroys the status quo.

Foxes will breed once each year and are sexually mature when ten months old. But then only the dominant vixen will come into season, into oestrus, and only for a short time, usually in January. During this period the dog and vixen call more regularly, with the male being a perfect suitor, always close to his betrothed, playing with her and grooming her. Copulation may take place on many occasions, with the pair often lying back to back as so often seen with dogs. There are only three days during oestrus when the vixen may be fertilised; if this occurs a pregnancy of fifty-three days will follow.

Other vixens may display 'phantom pregnancies' and some outside a family group may fall pregnant to itinerant males, but these pregnancies generally do not reach fruition, though occasionally two vixens in an area may produce litters and rear them in the same earth, or in close proximity to each other.

The cubs, four or five of them, are usually born in March. They are blind, deaf and covered in short black fur, looking more like kittens than foxes. The vixen is a devoted mother and will not leave the earth for two weeks, relying on her spouse and the non-breeding vixens to bring her food. The indiscriminate killing of foxes may cause unseen hardship, depriving the vixen of her food supply.

As the cubs grow and are weaned, and venture out of the earth, the whole family will provide them with solid or regurgitated food. They remain together until the end of September, by which time they will have grown to be replicas of their parents. Then they will disperse to find their own territories, with males travelling further than the females, some of which will remain with the family group as non-breeding vixens.

The fox's senses

All foxes will call at various times of the year but, whether it is the loud, mating screams of the vixen or the short, muffled bark of a mother warning her cubs of danger, only the fox's superb hearing will be able to decipher its meaning. A fox's ears are its radio antennae. They not only pick up every call and rustle, but enable the fox to pinpoint with some accuracy the position of another fox, or a prey animal, or even a predator. Watch how a fox listens and see how it moves its head slightly to get a bearing on the sound it is concentrating on. The slightest rustle or squeak could point to a mouse or vole up to a hundred metres away. Humans could not possibly hear such a minute sound; we have to be content with only a glimpse of the

Above *A fox's ears are its radio antennae*
Left *The foxes eyes reflect light*

foxes' world of sound through their calling to each other: the true 'call of the wild'.

However, I would imagine that most of us have, just for a moment, also glimpsed the green glow of a fox's eyes reflected in the car headlights as it disappears once more into the darkness of the night. It is not, in fact, the fox's eyes themselves which glow, but a light-reflecting layer, the *tapetum lucidum*, at the back of the eye, which reflects your headlights back at you. Diurnal animals, creatures of the day, normally have a light-absorbing, pigmented schorid at the back of the eye, whereas those with the benefit of a *tapetum lucidum* are able to increase the light directed onto the retina by reflecting it back through the eye, using it twice. This enables any nocturnal or crepuscular animal to see far better in poor light conditions. To increase further its ability to see in these conditions, the fox has in its retina an increased number of the photoreceptors called rods, cells which are stimulated by poor light. As a result, it has fewer of the photoreceptors called cones, cells which discern the finer details of an image. Because of this lack of fine detail perception it is said that foxes cannot discern stationary objects or people, but just one tiny movement makes them aware and reacting in an instant. This lack of cones, which are thought to be the colour receptors of the eye, also means that foxes, like most mammals, are probably colour blind.

A fox's eyes are generally a bright yellow-brown, although for the first four weeks after its birth the cub's eyes are blue. Unlike all other members of the *Canidae*, except the kit fox, the fox's pupils contract into a slit, rather like a cat's eyes, and quite unlike the other dogs', whose pupils remain rounded as they contract in the light.

But even with imperfect eyesight, the fox still has its superb hearing and two other senses that enable it to be master of its environment. These are the super-senses of smell and touch. The fox obviously also has a sense of taste, shown by its preferences for certain species of vole over other species of mice and shrews, but his is probably as primitive as our own sense of taste and has little effect on its lifestyle. Its sense of smell, on the other hand, is a super-sense, a lifeline to survival. That long pointed snout directs every whiff or flicker of smell back onto the well-developed olfactory lobes, the part of the brain that deciphers the messages passed by the nose. Humans have poorly developed olfactory lobes so we cannot even contemplate the sophisticated images foxes instinctively create from the slightest scents around them. Perhaps the picture is somewhat like that produced by the heat-seeking cameras of the fire brigade and other rescue teams. Having met many of the larger British mammals – foxes and badgers – I am convinced that the scent pictures seen

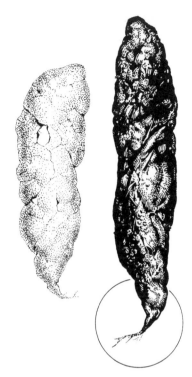

Fox droppings, left *old* right *fresh, actual size*

by these animals are indelibly imprinted on their memory, rather as we recall images we have seen in the past.

The fox lives in a world of scented images, which could be a cache of food buried in its form of a larder, or a titbit buried deep in a tightly sealed rubbish bag, or the aromatic signposts left around its territory by itself or other foxes. On the regular circuits that a fox makes of its territory, it will leave its calling card of urine or faeces in prominent positions, on a stump or a mound, for instance, as notice to other foxes that 'this territory is spoken for'. As it empties one of its food caches, the fox will scent-mark it as empty, saving a fruitless effort in digging it up. Some of these scent-marks are so pungent that they can even register on a human's paltry scenting scale.

The fox produces this very strong scent in its urine; it is also deposited on its faeces as they pass the anal gland. Foxes also have other glands that impart more subtle aromas, mostly undetectable by humans but presumably still of great importance in the fox world. On the undersides of their feet they have small scent glands, the purpose of which we can only imagine. These leave a scent in the fox's footprints – a dead giveaway to bumbling foxhounds. The other important gland is the supra-caudal gland that shows as a small, black mark about a third of the way down the tail, or brush. It is said that the secretion from this gland fluoresces under ultraviolet light and has the rather pleasant, sweet smell of violets, giving it the alternative name of 'violet gland'.

We can only make assumptions as to the purpose of all these glandular secretions, and their value in the fox's scented world, but I believe that we can be more certain of the purpose of the fox's whiskers, the *vibrissae*. They serve a touch-sensitive purpose, assisting the fox's other senses, especially at night. These *vibrissae* are black and situated on the muzzle, around the eyes, on the chin and along both forelegs. The main *vibrissae* on the muzzle have a combined width of over eleven centimetres, making them wider than the fox's body and enabling it to feel the width of a gap before it passes through, rather as a car driver relies on his wing mirrors to calculate a passing space.

All of these senses – sight, hearing, smell and touch – combine instinctively to give the fox an instant 'printout' of its surroundings in the split second that's so essential for survival. Rather than living by its wits and cunning, as some would have us believe, the fox therefore relies on its super-senses, perfectly tuned to its nocturnal, hunting lifestyle.

The fox's body

The more tangible aspects of a fox's body have also evolved superbly to enable the fox to cope with its lifestyle. As I have mentioned in Chapter 2, the long bones of its front legs are fused to facilitate fleetness of movement over open ground. Its feet are designed so that the fox walks on the soft, round pads at the tips of its toes, making it a digitigrade animal rather than a plantigrade

Fox tracks, left *fore foot,* right *hind foot, actual size*

(like the hedgehog), which walks with its feet flat to the ground. The fox has five toes on each front foot, although the dew claw is rarely seen in any paw prints. If a paw print defiantly shows five toes, the four-toed hind paw has probably been placed in the mark of the foreprint and has overlapped. The underside of the fox's toes are naked (except in the Arctic fox, which has hair covering the underside of its toes), but there is fur in between each toe, which may show on a paw print in very soft ground.

As a fox is walking or trotting it leaves a straight track as the prints of the hind paws overlap the front paw prints. At a walking pace the length of the track between paw prints is about thirty centimetres, stretching to sixty centimetres as it changes to a trotting gait. At full gallop, at about sixty-five kilometres per hour, the fox's tracks are extended up to 300 centimetres apart, with its feet placed more or less side by side.

While a fox can run at sixty-five kilometres per hour, it can do so only for short distances. It may be able to walk or trot for mile after mile, but at full gallop, as it would be in front of hounds, it would be exhausted in no time at all.

Foxhounds are bred to be able to run long distances and have an unfair advantage over any unfortunate quarry fox, both in size and staying power.

Foxes obtain their larger prey by short, sharp sprints rather like a cheetah, relying on surprise as well as speed. Small prey items, like voles, are caught with front feet after a typical fox pounce, learned from the time it was six weeks old. The vole is pinned to the ground by the front feet, while the jaws deliver a quick *coup de grâce*. The advantage of this method of hunting is that should the fox miss with its feet, then it has a second chance to catch its escaping prey with its mouth and razor-sharp canine teeth.

I know the canine teeth are razor-sharp as I have been slashed across the hand by a fox rather than being bitten. The canines are generally used for capturing prey, while the shearing, carnassial teeth are used to crush and tear it into smaller pieces. A carnivore's jaw has no sideways movement to allow food to be chewed. Instead, the food is chopped or bitten into pieces and swallowed. Their digestive system is geared to this method of feeding by having very short intestines and a vestigial caecum, quite the opposite of some of their herbivorous prey.

A full complement of teeth numbers forty-two, noticeably two molars fewer than might be expected (although a third pair of molars in the top jaw may sometimes be present). The dental formula of a fox used by scientists to identify a species is:

3.1.4.2 3 incisors, 1 canine, 4 premolars, 2 molars on each side of
      the top jaw
3.1.4.3 3 incisors, 1 canine, 4 premolars, 3 molars on each side of
      the bottom jaw

Provided a fox has a good complement of healthy unbroken teeth it can, in Britain, reach a weight of nearly eight kilograms (for a vixen) or some nine kilograms (for a male). However these larger weights tend to be seen only in Scottish foxes; in England and Wales vixens average about 5.4 kilograms and males about 6.7 kilograms, barely larger than a domestic cat.

Like the cat, the fox has a fine coat of fur which not only keeps it dry but also protects it from cold weather conditions. However, unlike the domestic cat which moults at odd times because it lives in an artificial, centrally heated environment, the fox moults just once a year beginning mostly in late April when the short hairs of the feet are lost. The moult progresses to the rump and tail and finally to the shoulders and face. After the short underfur falls out the longer guard hairs soon follow only to be replaced by a much shorter sleeker coat for the summer. This coat continues to grow slowly until, by the autumn, the fox has its typical thick coat ready to face the rigours of winter. (Sarcoptic mange, which I will describe in Chapter 7, also causes the hair to fall out, beginning with the rump and presenting a raw, scabby, hairless appearance which should not be confused with a typical moult.)

All told, the fox is perfectly proportioned and superbly equipped for its hunting/scavenging existence. Sometimes it does encroach on man's environment, often sidestepping slipshod defences to take advantage of any bounty offered. This is nowadays only a rare occurrence, for the fox generally uses its expertise to survive in its own wild world. In so doing it often indirectly brings benefits to the very people whose hands are raised against it.

CHAPTER FOUR

LIVING WITH FOXES

The fox as predator

Despite being equipped with the most sophisticated sensory resources evolution can provide, and being armed with formidable teeth, jaws and claws, the life of a predator is still very precarious. Though decreed by nature to cull the weak, sick or dying, it is still not very easy to hunt another animal which, even if sick, has itself a complete set of techniques geared to avoid capture. Yet life for the recognised prey species is comparatively simple. With no conceptions that it may be the subject of a hunter's attention, the prey carries on eating and breeding oblivious until that instant when the predator strikes. And even then the odds are such that it will escape. Take the rabbit, for instance – it leaves its burrow to find the food which grows all around it just waiting to be eaten. It sees a fox walking through the colony just as an antelope in Africa may see a lion walking through its herd. The rabbit knows instinctively whether the fox is hunting or not and will generally ignore it, carrying on munching oblivious until that moment when the fox becomes alert, and even then the rabbit's reaction is not fear but an instant urgency to gain the safety of its bolt hole. If the fox successfully takes the rabbit, the drama is over in the swift moment it takes the predator to despatch its prey. The killing of an animal seems horrific to us, but once again nature has decreed that it is done as humanely as possible.

The main prey animal of foxes in the British Isles has always been the **rabbit** but in the two years 1954–6 disaster struck as man introduced that most horrible of viral diseases, myxomatosis. Thankfully for other animal species the disease only affects rabbits. Within months 99.9 per cent of the vast rabbit population was either dead or dying. True, as they fell sick or dying the stricken rabbits became easy prey for foxes and other predators who for a short time thrived on this bonanza. But then, as swiftly as it had arrived, the epidemic ran its course and nearly all the rabbits had gone, either eaten, decomposed, or burned on huge funeral pyres by distraught farmers who, although they fought a constant battle against rabbits, were devastated by the efficient cruelty of the myxomatosis virus.

Predatory animals like the fox, stoat and buzzard who had spent centuries perfecting their techniques of catching rabbits now, all of a sudden, had nothing to hunt. The stoat and buzzard nearly succumbed to the paucity and their numbers plummeted, even though the stoat had enough guile to turn its attention to other live prey like grey squirrels, this was still not enough to maintain a buoyant population.

The farmers panicked, imagining that foxes would turn their attentions to livestock. After all, for years they had persecuted the fox, accusing it of taking their poultry, lambs and even piglets when they must have known that their victims were, in fact, helping them out by living predominantly on the number one crop-eaters: rabbits. Perhaps now was the time for retribution, with the foxes wreaking revenge for those years of atrocity. But no! I like to think that foxes ignored the gauntlet and sought another source of food.

The undoubted secret of the fox's survival over the years lies in its resourcefulness and adaptability, both of which were needed in the wake of myxomatosis more than ever before. This challenge the fox took up. Foxes turned to living on earthworms, fruit, birds and any carrion they could find lying around and, although I hate to admit it, did pay occasional visits to hen-houses when these were abundant before battery-farming became the norm.

They discovered bird tables, cat bowls, rubbish dumps and surprise, surprise, with the rabbits gone the grass, unnibbled, started to grow and grow, providing a perfect breeding habitat for the smaller mammals: **voles, wood-mice** and **shrews**. The fox was quick to exploit these new multitudes, even discriminating against the mice and shrews in favour of bank voles. Even today, forty years later, bank voles are the mainstay of the diet of adult foxes, in spite of the rabbit's recovery to almost pre-myxomatosis population levels.

Once more the farmers are coming under pressure from rabbits who are now eating into the vast acres of profits available through existing agricultural policies. Innocently the foxes are coming to the farmer's assistance by gradually reverting to their penchant for rabbit dinners. Yet many farmers still carry a cudgel with which to kill foxes, though the old conflict about raiding hen-houses is a thing of the past and the fox's reputation for slaying lambs is predominantly a figment of the imagination.

Foxes do occasionally take live **lambs**, but the numbers are small, probably about 0.5 per cent, one lamb in 200, and that is among the poorly protected, well-scattered flocks on the Welsh hillsides. Sheep on lowland farms enjoy much closer supervision so we would expect the numbers lost to be much smaller. All told, far more lambs are lost to dogs, particularly sheepdogs, than to any other form of predation.

The cost of tracking down and killing suspect foxes far outweighs the economic value of the animals lost, quite apart from the devastation and destitution inflicted on fox families who can never recover their personal losses.

The lamb myths all stem from the fox's habit of taking larger food items to its cubs at the earth, so cutting out several energy-sapping trips with small items of prey. Lamb carcasses and wool have often been found at the mouth of earths containing cubs – irrefutable proof that the fox has been killing lambs. Or is it? Could the carcass have been a lamb that died of natural causes before the fox found it? Surely there is enough reasonable doubt to stay the death sentence so liberally meted out for a 'crime' that is supported only by circumstantial evidence.

The fox may be the master opportunist but he is not foolishly brave and any ewe worth her salt will soon see off any fox that might approach her lamb. A study carried out in Australia proved that aggressive behaviour in a ewe and its readiness to stand up and stamp at an intruder – dog, fox, or man – is indicative of its physical condition and, if it has a lamb, of its ability to protect and nurture it. Failure to do this is indicative of the reverse: a ewe in poor condition, with a lamb which in consequence is probably undernourished and waiting to be taken. There you have

A healthy ewe will see off a fox

it. Any lamb carcasses found at cubbing earths were of either dead or dying lambs, the result, dare I say it, of poor husbandry where the ewe was not fit enough to protect her lamb or nourish it.

The other evening I heard bleating outside my study window. I went to investigate and found a ewe with two lambs which had strayed from a neighbouring farm. Rather than flee as a sheep would normally do, this ewe showed the courage of motherhood and actually charged down my torch beam. This convinced me that a fit ewe would have little trouble in seeing off a fox.

Many farmers actively believe that without controlling all potential predators (and that includes dogs and eagles, as well as foxes) they would lose 8.3 per cent of their lambs to foxes alone. This figure emanates I believe from a survey carried out in 1972, on behalf of the National Farmers Union, in the west of Scotland. The presumption of the first part of the survey appears to have been that if the number of ewes which should have had lambs with them but didn't was assessed, and the number of lambs found dead was then subtracted, any missing lambs must have been lost to predation. No allowance was apparently made for dead lambs not found by shepherds, though in the wilds of West Scotland carcasses could remain undiscovered in peat bogs, over cliffs, in tall vegetation, or in water, as well as being scavenged by foxes or eagles. The fox was the natural scapegoat for something which could, after all, have been the result of poor animal husbandry or harsh weather conditions. This information came to light in a report by Ray Hewson, entitled *Victim of Myth*, published in 1990 by the League Against Cruel Sports.

In order to nullify or justify the claims that fox predation has a serious economic effect, particularly on hill farms in Scotland and Wales, Dr Ray Hewson of the University of Aberdeen was commissioned to spend three years investigating the effect of not controlling foxes on an estate in the north of Scotland. Being a methodical scientist he monitored a neighbouring estate where control was still practised, as a comparison for his findings.

Dr Hewson proved that the control of foxes had no beneficial effect on the numbers of lambs raised, although it did have serious repercussions for the foxes and their families. His overall conclusion was that the number of dead sheep left unattended during the winter and available as carrion enabled the fox population to flourish. If landowners wanted to reduce the fox numbers, which was not entirely necessary, then as Dr Hewson puts it: 'Improvement in management leading to fewer dead sheep might reduce the fox population more than the current methods of control.'

Foxes are often guilty of hanging around lambing fields in the lambing season but they are inevitably scavenging the afterbirth material before the ewes themselves eat it. An afterbirth from a sheep can weigh half a kilogram, which is half an adult fox's normal daily food requirement and a good meal for many small cubs. As most sheep give birth over a short period then the amount of afterbirth available is more than enough to satisfy the needs of quite a few foxes for many days. After all, in true fox tradition, any surplus can be cached for eating at a later date and foxes do not seem to mind how long it may have been buried. During those first few vulnerable days of a lamb's life, its supposed arch enemy will be so replete on the easy options it has been able to scavenge that it is highly unlikely it will attempt a confrontation with an irate ewe; so healthy new-born lambs can be regarded as safe from the fox's attention.

This business of identifying carcasses and meat outside the cubbing earth and then condemning the fox parents as the killers of these animals is, to me, fraught with error. Take, for instance, the remains of a New Forest pony found at an earth, and the numerous records of cattle portions found in similar circumstances. In my work at the Hospital I encounter many foxes but even I would be reluctant to handle a fox that could kill a pony, or a cow.

It seems to me that since that 1972 survey, lamb-killing has become the farmers' bugbear, replacing the old image of the fox forever raiding hen-houses in the time when **chickens** were allowed some life and freedom instead of being, as they are now, incarcerated in small metal prisons where they can never scratch the soil for seeds, feel the sun and rain, or even encounter a fox, which would surely be a price worth paying.

Free-range chicken farms are now on the increase and those running them realise they are going to receive close attention from their neighbourhood foxes. So they take

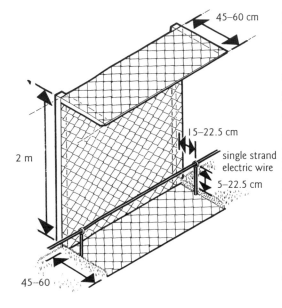

45–60 cm

15–22.5 cm

single strand electric wire

5–22.5 cm

2 m

45–60

Fox-proof fencing

precautions. They erect fox-proof fencing. They make sure their hen-houses are secure and if their birds do roost outside they provide only perches that are high enough to be out of reach. I have even heard how one henkeeper clipped the lower branches of his trees and shrubs so that his chickens had to roost high and safely. The henkeepers are careful – and suffer no losses to the local foxes.

The cost of re-fencing a garden hen-yard or a small-holding is expensive, but as long as you make sure that the hen-house is secure, with a good sturdy door locked top and bottom, and you round up your birds every evening, you should have no trouble. The chicken runs or duck pens can even be made fox-proof during the day by surrounding them with electric fencing, which is surprisingly cheap and easy to erect. It is not a danger to foxes or other animals and if set properly will deter any intruder with a low voltage jolt. One point though – please keep the lower strands of the fence at least fifteen centimetres (six inches) from the ground or hedgehogs may become tragically trapped; whereas other animals will simply touch the wire and recoil, a hedgehog curls into a ball and receives shock after shock after shock until it dies of exhaustion, starvation, or heart failure.

Any chickens should now be secure. But what if a fox does get through your defences and into your hen-house? Sadly it may kill more than the one bird it carries away. 'They kill for fun, you know!' – I can hear the character assassination already. Of course they do not kill for fun, only man has that dubious distinction when he is hunting or blasting away at fat, round pheasants who can hardly get off the ground. Yes, foxes do kill more than they can either eat or carry away in one go, but this is the intuitive act of any predator when offered easy pickings like chickens confined in a small area. It's like us going to a supermarket in a free-for-all and grabbing all that we can while the price is low.

Take a tiger, for instance. It may well kill a deer too large to eat at one sitting. It will eat some that day and save the rest for another day. Usually, it manages to carry off its prize, whereas a fox could not possibly carry off numerous chickens in one go. It will take the first chicken to its cubs, then return to collect more of its prize which it can cache in its foxy larders. The only difference is that the fox never gets a chance to return to the supermarket as the misdemeanour will, by then, have been discovered and pandemonium broken loose.

This is perfectly normal predator behaviour but nobody condemns the tiger, lion, or bear for killing more than it can eat. Incidentally those other old wives' tales about a fox carrying off a goose over its shoulder make no sense, as a goose would be far too heavy. Just as ludicrous is the farmer living near us who insisted that a fox killed and carried off his six-kilogram piglets. Most foxes themselves do not weigh six kilograms so I cannot see how it would have been possible, unless the pony-killer from the New Forest has been making forays into Buckinghamshire.

Sometimes foxes take the blame for other intruders, even being accused after other raiders have decimated the hen-house. Buckinghamshire is renowned for badgers breaking through all defences. And in Skye, Paul and Grace Yoxon, who run the Skye Environmental Centre (where Sue and I are patrons), have to contend with marauding otters. Even rats can cause havoc among poultry, but rest assured that the faeces of a visiting fox are supposed to be a surefire rat deterrent.

I have mentioned the shooting of pheasants. It's the management of **game birds** and estates for shooting by gamekeepers that is one of the most ominous threats to foxes, and any other carnivores for that matter. Actually, free-living partridges and pheasants fare no worse at the hands of foxes than other potential prey species in the countryside. Because pheasants roost high in bushes and trees and nest sporadically, they do not suffer any significant losses – the motor car is a far more serious threat than foxes. Partridges, on the other hand, have a different lifestyle and can meet problems especially during nesting seasons. But nature was aware of this, giving partridges tremendous egg-laying capabilities to offset any losses due to predation – rather like the rabbit's ability to breed rapidly and recover *its* natural losses. That's the whole point – these species can recover from natural losses but just as rabbit numbers plummeted through myxomatosis, so partridge populations have been decimated by agricultural chemicals and now they feel the effect of just a few fox incidents.

And even though numbers are low the guns still blast away at any partridge that puts its head above the grass.

Gamekeepers are now rearing more partridges to shoot, with their main concern being that the fox will raid their rearing pens stuffed full, as they are, with native grey partridges plus alien pheasants and red-legged partridges. Just like the hen-house crammed with chickens the rearing pens are an artificial bonanza if the fox can get in. Can you blame him? The gamekeepers have their own methods of protecting the precious cannon-fodder birds, based on the 'shoot on sight' principle. They do not seem to have realised that, if you kill one fox, a vacant territory is created, an open invitation for another fox or foxes to move in. Then *they* have to be killed, and so it goes on.

A fox family has its own territory which no other fox will be allowed to enter. On the open hillsides this territory could run to 1,000 hectares while on lowland farms and estates it could be 200–300 hectares. While the fox family is in occupation there will be set, invisible boundaries. Killing those foxes will open those boundaries and who knows how many foxes will move into the vacuum.

The fox's food

In spite of the stories the critics will bandy about, the fox actually spends most of its life seeking out a wild diet. From various zoological studies it has been proven that the fox shows a preference for bank voles and rabbits, but it will take any opportunity offered, especially preying on pigeons and other birds when living in an urban environment. Even in the cities the fox silently helps out by taking rats and mice, especially in Ireland where there was no vole population to replace the myxomatosis rabbits. David Macdonald, the well-known fox-watcher, points out that a fox can exist on 240 earthworms a night. Invertebrates including beetles, caterpillars and other insects are regularly topped up with carrion, fruit and even fish, if the fox can catch them. He will eat practically anything as one lady henkeeper found out. Being sensible she made her hen-houses impregnable only to find that her neighbourhood fox turned its attention to her orchard. The old fable about the fox and the grapes has almost become reality, with the British fox relishing such fruit as apples, pears, raspberries, bilberries, sloes, cherries and – its particular favourite – blackberries, which it picks carefully by standing upright on its hind legs to avoid the bramble thorns. No doubt in France and other wine-producing countries the vineyards are on many foxes' itineraries.

Many surveys have been carried out on fox diets mainly, it seems, by dissecting the stomach remains of dead foxes. Indigestible silver paper and food wrappers are common, together with elastic bands and even contraceptives, but never any grasshoppers. Apparently, even with their super-sense of hearing, foxes, just like we humans, are unable to locate these strident insects.

Unfortunately as more foxes desert the barren countryside to take up an urban existence the townspeople's unprotected pet rabbits and guinea pigs do face some risk of being taken. As with free-living chickens the fox will be quick to take advantage of any chink in your pet's armour. There are now fox populations in Bristol, Oxford, Edinburgh, Glasgow and most towns. I even know of a pair of foxes that live in Brixton in the heart of London. There are likely to be foxes in your neighbourhood so take precautions with your rabbits and guinea pigs – make sure that their hutches are safe and secure, supervise them when they are running free around the garden and put a secure wire roof over any exercise pens.

Dogs are at no risk from foxes, though conversely the foxes themselves are often attacked and killed by dogs. Cats are probably the supreme predators, with a frightening array of weapons, armed tooth and claw. Most foxes are only a little larger than cats and appreciate that they risk being injured should they even attempt aggression towards these formidable night prowlers. Fox and cat often meet and generally ignore each other's presence, although occasionally a cat may send a fox packing or vice versa. Once again cat fur has been found in fox faeces and at cubbing earths but most likely these are the remains of road traffic victims scavenged by the fox.

In this new urban environment foxes are regularly accused of overturning dustbins or ripping open rubbish bags. It is not necessarily true – most of these misdemeanours are the work of dogs, cats, badgers, or even squirrels – but, as we have seen so many times, the fox is the scapegoat again.

The fox-friendly garden

People in towns and suburbs are often worried by the presence of a fox or its family in their garden. The fear has, over the years, been compounded by some local councils which have had no hesitation in sending in the pest control operatives who seem to know only one remedy – slaughter. It has been proven time and again

Watching a cub in your garden is a joy

that foxes are not a danger: they are not disease-ridden and in my experience are probably the cleanest of all British wild mammals. A friend of mine, Trevor Williams, is now trying to remedy the situation. He has set up a service called Fox Project with a policy of providing advice to landowners and councils on fox questions. It's everybody's right to say 'yea' or 'nay' to foxes on their property, but Trevor's use of advice, experience and harmless repellents has enabled unwanted foxes to be moved on without resorting to the gun.

There are many repellents on the market but do be careful as some, like creosote, can actually harm the animals.

It is a well-known fact that if a vixen nursing cubs suspects any disturbance she will carry her charges to a new earth. If you really do not want a fox earth in your garden you could try a little gentle dissuasion like planting a peppermint bush or garlic plant just outside the entrance. Conversely if you want your foxes to stay do not disturb them in any way and that includes no putting food at the earth entrance.

On the other hand, if you would like the privilege of foxes in your garden, why not make it fox-friendly: leave a gap under the garden shed where a vixen can have her cubs. There is nothing more enchanting in wildlife than watching newly weaned fox cubs gambolling in the early morning light: a sight that has turned many a fox-hater into a fox-lover overnight. Your neighbourhood fox has already probably discovered your bird table but why not, at night, put out a bowl of dog food or kitchen scraps – even if the fox does not take it a hedgehog or cat might. Incidentally, foxes pose no threat to most hedgehogs,

Encourage foxes by making your garden fox-friendly

preferring not to run the gauntlet of those spines.

I receive many letters from people who are thrilled to have foxes in their gardens, and I hear many enthusiastic stories, but the classic must be a recent phone call. A lady had been putting out tinned dog food for her visiting fox. This was fine until the fox tried to take some away, presumably to cubs nearby. Obviously it could not pick up the mushy dog food. Not to be outdone, it somehow cottoned on to the fact that if it removed two slices of bread from the bird feeder it could carry the dog food in a foxy version of a sandwich. I am assured that this is true and if so it proves once and for all that it's intuitive opportunism that makes foxes so resilient.

Encourage foxes into your garden. They are enchanting, clean, handsome neighbours. In return for your hospitality, they will dispose of nasty garden pests as well as any mice or rats, which I now understand are on the increase in and around most towns.

CHAPTER FIVE
'TEAR 'IM, EAT 'IM'

As most foxes around the world have evolved similar habits I have, in many places, assumed a broad-spectrum view of their lifestyle and habits. In this chapter I had hoped to provide a strong, yet sound and reasonable comment on the various guises of fox persecution in different countries, while endeavouring to maintain a level and unemotional attitude to foxhunting with hounds. I have tried and tried, but have found it impossible, so I apologise if some emotion creeps into the next few pages.

I have sat at my desk for days on end trying to remain aloof and unmoved but now every conscious moment seems to be filled with images I have witnessed or read about of atrocities committed against foxes – not in Bolivia or Manchuria or Outer Mongolia but here, in Britain, our supposedly green and pleasant land.

Yesterday I walked among the fox cubs in the Hospital, wondering about their future back in the wild. Even the arrival of the first baby hedgehogs of the season failed to lift my desperate depression. I had been finding out about the foxhunts, week in and week out before the season had even started and it was haunting me.

Cub-hunting

I had always understood, and we are all regularly told, that cub-hunting is a way of dispersing that year's young foxes around the countryside. That does not seem to create too much of a hardship although renowned fox-watcher Dr Stephen Harris has shown that fox cubs which have been dispersed are more susceptible to accident or control measures, and can spread disease, if there is any present. But in actual fact cub-hunting has little or nothing to do with dispersal – we have all been hoodwinked by hunting propaganda.

We also believe that foxhunting has tradition and pageantry that have been handed down for centuries. When I tell you that approximately 50 per cent of all hunting kills are made at dawn before the hunting season even opens on November the first, and that the vast majority of the hunt followers, together with their tradition and pageantry, are not invited to attend, you can begin to see that the hunting propaganda has something to hide.

Between August and October the huntsmen, hounds and a few invited guests surreptitiously creep out before dawn for mornings of cub-hunting. The dates and times are not publicised or shown on the hunt calendar. There are dark and dirty deeds to be done and the fewer that know about it, the better.

My shocked enlightening was from the report by the late Robert Churchward, a Master of Hounds, whose heart was broken by an orphaned fox cub handed to him by a small boy after it had survived a typical hunting massacre of a vixen and her family. It does not make pretty reading but it is the truth and I would ask you to steel yourselves

Four orphans spared the horrors of cub-hunting

and read it for the sake of foxes and cubs to come. A brief extract follows:

> We made for the small wood where, the Master had been informed, there was a litter of cubs. First of all he ordered the 30 or so people out that morning to surround the wood.
>
> Then he sent hounds and Hunt staff into the thickets inside the circle of waiting horsemen and women.
>
> At first nothing happened. Then the hounds' baying told us that the litter had been found. I waited to see what happened.
>
> As the cubs were frightened away from their mother they ran desperately out of the wood, only to be frightened back into the very jaws of the hounds.
>
> It was nothing more than a circle of death. People on horseback holloaed at the tops of their voices, flapped their reins and banged the sides of their leather saddles with their hunting crops.
>
> They set up such an unholy clamour that the second the frightened cub ran out of his home and, as he thought, out of danger, he was frightened back.
>
> Hounds ate every cub. At one stage I was disgusted to see the pups whipped away from the older hounds and a fox cub chased into their inexpert mouths by the Master's command

of, 'Let the pups have that one.'

It was a terrible scene. The pups, lacking the experience of the older hounds, were not quite sure how to deal with the cub.

They bit the cub and were bitten back. They treated it as both something to kill and something to play with. There was a sordid scuffle in which fur, flesh and blood flew in all directions.

After what seemed like an hour – actually it was only a few minutes – there was nothing left of the cub.

The pups looked up proudly, wagging their sterns (you never call them tails) and waited for praise from their Master.

This was the pups' education.

He adds:

Let me say this bluntly from my 40 years' experience of the sport: The main reason for cubbing [an alternative term for cub-hunting] is to educate the young hounds by letting them eat live cubs.

How can any human being be a party to this? These innocent victims may be called fox cubs but they are in reality young puppies. Foxes are dogs of the same family, the *Canidae*, as our favourite pooches. They have the same loyalties and emotions we have all grown to appreciate in our own dogs. Would we allow our puppies to be tortured and eaten, yes eaten, in this barbaric manner? One of fox-hunting's better images was that it decreed a close season to allow foxes to breed unhindered. Now we know why. It is to provide fodder on which to train stale or inexperienced hounds how to eat others of a similar species; they need to be trained because it is totally unnatural.

Some hunts even provide artificial earths just to make sure that there are foxes available. And that's not all – any hound that shows distaste for the kill is shot, along with others that disobey orders. In fact in hunting circles each year about 16,000 hounds are shot and killed (and supposedly fed to the other hounds); a far greater mortality than the estimated 12–13,000 foxes killed annually by those same hunts.

The whole grisly subject is wallowing in the blood of foxes and hounds. I am at a loss for suitable words that could be printed. What inhumanity will our orphaned fox cubs suffer when we release them?

We have quite a few cubs in at the moment. Most of them are orphans whose mothers, fathers, brothers and sisters have been killed, mostly, I might add, by accident, for this is the close season before August the first. As you walk into our Large Mammal Ward the rows of bright eyes look appealingly towards you.

In the first cage are BP and Willy with their heads lying side by side on their cuddly panda.

Wingnut in the next cage is all ears. Her fur has been ravaged by mange but she is recovering slowly. Her ears stand erect as you approach, looking for comfort. We dare not give her any attention as we must keep her wild. And she doesn't understand that in three weeks, when her mange is cleared, she will be able to mix with the other orphans.

Wingnut who must be kept apart at present

Peewee, in the next cage, comes to the front and whimpers for attention. We must not handle her, she must stay wild. She is tiny,

Rambo, with his leg in plaster

dwarfed by her toy clown as she cuddles down once more, baffled at being rejected again. She has a tummy upset and has to stay on her own for a few days.

Beneath her is Rambo. He is the toughie fox cub, or at least he tries to be. His leg is in plaster from a car accident. He spits and snarls, ears back just like an adult fox's, but he is so small you can't help but smile at his bravado.

There are others. They are all safe. They all have sad eyes and sad barks and they make me want to keep them and protect them for ever, but I must not succumb. They are wild animals and are entitled to a wild existence. At least I will make sure they are fully grown and strong before they meet the outside world. They may then stand a chance if a foxhunt happens to trespass on their territory. Or will they?

Foxhunting myths
There are many myths about foxhunting, such as that it is an age-old British tradition, or that if the hunt does keep up with the fox, the fox is killed quickly and humanely. These are quite divorced from the real, unsavoury facts.

To start with, foxhunting as we know it is not a centuries-old tradition. It has only been around for 250 years and only came about because the deer and hares, which were the real traditional quarry, were becoming scarce, presumably due to deforestation, persecution and the after-effects of the Civil War. Hunting the fox, in those days, was regarded as a 'crude sport' that meant 'little more than riding and running'.

Nowadays there is a lot of colour, ceremony and dressing up as the hunt swill their stirrup cups. It's picturesque, in an old-fashioned Christmas card sort of way, as they clatter off on their high horses, but look behind the bright columns and notice the men in the dowdy brown and green Land-Rovers bringing up the rear. These are the real heart, if that's the right word, of fox hunting, the terrier men who, by fair means or foul, make sure that there is a fox to be killed at the end of the chase. These are the huntsmen who never appear on any Christmas card, the Bill Sykeses who do all the dirty work and go unseen and unheralded on the glamorous occasions in the hunt calendar.

The columns of horses and hollering hounds may be lucky enough to put up a fox and pelt at literally breakneck speed after it, but a fox has not evolved for a long chase and at the first opportunity it heads for a likely underground retreat. This is its nature and its instinctive reaction to danger – to find what should be a sure means of escape. It would escape too, except that the terrier men have been out the night before and blocked every drain, rabbit burrow, badger set or just plain hole, so that nothing can get in or out.

The fox is forced to run until it is exhausted, all the time knowing that the hounds, huntsmen and tootling horns are right behind him, driving him on until he drops. To quote Robert Churchward again, since he has been there where, thank God, I have not:

> We had left the Hunt an hour before and were dawdling along towards the village of Armitage when, on rounding a sharp bend in the road, I had a clear and close view of a nearly beaten fox.
>
> It dragged itself painfully and slowly through the blackthorn hedge and squeezed wearily through the gate on the other side of the road. The animal was a lightly built vixen and was obviously reaching the end of its tether.
>
> With ears laid back to catch the sound of pursuit, it tottered a few steps into the field, trailing its bedraggled brush along the ground.
>
> Its eyes were glazed and its tongue lolled out. Then it sank, exhausted, into a plough furrow, its breath coming in great heaving gasps.
>
> Suddenly I became aware of the approach of the hounds. They rounded the side of the wood in full cry. Staccato toots of the hunting horn and the beat and thud of the horses' hooves echoed all around me.
>
> Round the bend they came and into the field. Now the fox was in the hounds' full view.
>
> Their cries rose in savage triumph. The leading hounds flung themselves onto the half-dead fox, seizing it wherever they could get a grip with their fangs.
>
> The animal made one last desperate attempt to rise. Each fresh hound as it came up tried with might and main to sink its teeth into some portion of the fox's body.
>
> Rending, tearing, snarling, growling, biting and ripping, the hounds swirled in a circle around the doomed quarry.
>
> Each late arrival leaped into the middle of the circle of death in a frantic effort to get a grip on the dying fox. Sometimes a hound got hold of another hound in the frenzy. Yelps of pain added to the macabre turmoil.

The scene is not difficult to imagine. It is nightmarish

but only a few are aware of the sound-effects not obvious in those graphic black and white photographs of the kill. A well-known author, Caroline Blackwood, witnessed film of hunting kills and commented that her most vivid memories were of 'the high-pitched, child-like screams that the foxes let out as the hounds literally tore them to pieces'. The screams of those murdered foxes seemed to go on echoing around her head long after the films had ended. And I believe that Caroline Blackwood had started out to give an unbiased view of both sides of the hunting debate.

Where is the quick, clean kill we all hear about? It does not exist. Pack animals like wolves and hounds instinctively hunt larger animals carrying enough meat to feed that pack. Consequently it is numbers alone that can pull that animal down, the pack hunter is unlikely to use the *coup de grâce* bite to the neck or throat practised by the solitary hunter – the leopard, tiger, weasel, or fox. Any animal caught by a pack of anything is killed by a succession of bites and the fox at the mercy of a pack of hounds is no different. The body of one fox that was killed by the hounds was retrieved before it could be eaten by the pack and was taken to a veterinary surgeon for a post-mortem that would be beyond reproach. The report reads:

> I could detect no external damage to the neck and throat areas, but there were extensive wounds to the abdomen and thorax. In fact the abdomen was ripped open and the intestines were hanging out. The wounds were consistent with the fox being severely bitten by another animal or animals.

There have been many documented instances of injured pet dogs and cats being rescued alive from packs of foxhounds. If the 'instantaneous kill from the first bite' argument was true, they would have been dead, along with many other pets slaughtered by rampaging, out-of-control foxhounds and presumably all killed by being ripped to shreds. But then the huntsmen's cries as the fox is brought down are 'Tear 'im, eat 'im'; hardly commensurate with the quick, clean death we are all told about.

If the fox is lucky the huntsmen will retrieve it before it is torn asunder. The purpose? Nothing humanitarian. It is retrieved in order to kill it and cut off its head, its paws and its once proud tail, which are then presented to various guests of the hunt.

Any children witnessing their first kill are honoured by having the bloody, faeces-covered end of the poor fox's tail wiped around their faces. What a moment!

The hounds then get their reward and are frenzied by the huntsmen to eat the remainder of the fox, and then it is on to the next kill.

This, I hasten to add, has been the glamorous side of foxhunting – the pleasure that a few people pay a lot of money to be involved in. The real seamy side of foxhunting – yes, there is more – comes when the fleeing fox outwits the earth-stoppers and finds a bolt hole in the ground. This is when the nondescript brown and green terriermen move in to take their retribution on a fox that has the audacity to deny their Master his sport.

From the backs of the Land-Rovers come the terriermen's tools: small terriers, picks and shovels and, occasionally, a fox in a sack ready to give to the Master so that he can enjoy uninterrupted sport. This is the moment when laws are broken. Under the Protection of Animals Act 1911, a fox in a sack is deemed to be captive, the

Spitfire lost the end of his nose, perhaps to a spade

equivalent of a domestic animal. As such it is subject to the laws against cruelty whereas a wild animal has no protection. Releasing a 'bagged' fox in front of the hounds is illegal, hence you do not hear it mentioned in the propaganda. Some years ago I happened upon a foxhunt that was in the doldrums; then, lo and behold, a fox appeared from a sack and the hullabaloo started up again.

Terriermen have also been known to cut the fox's paws with a knife not only to produce a stronger, bloody scent for the hounds to follow but to provide a lame fox that is much easier to catch. Hamstringing the fox or breaking its bottom jaw are just two of the other techniques available if you want 'good' hunting.

Before the bagged fox is produced the small fearless terriers are put into the bolt hole in an attempt to make the fox run out in front of the hounds. If this does not happen the hunt riders will either move off or have a bagged fox to take them away, leaving the terriermen to the long-winded chore of digging the beleaguered fox out of its sanctuary.

By this time the fox underground is cornered and will turn and defend itself against the terriers. Both the dogs and the fox will get badly bitten but the terriermen look upon their terriers' scars as merits of battle, so they let the baiting continue.

Using the sounds of the battle as a pointer they dig down to retrieve the fox which is then supposedly shot, once again because the fox could be deemed to be captive and be subject to cruelty laws. However, I have heard that retrieved foxes have been thrown to the hounds, dead or alive, and have even been bagged for future sport.

Failure to obtain the fox is usually followed by the hole being filled in. There have been reported incidents of vixens and cubs, and even terriers, being buried alive.

I have just, for the second time, sat through hours of videotape filmed by the New Forest Animal Protection Group at digs in that once great woodland. In most instances the hounds and horses seemed to stay to witness the drawn-out spectacle of cloth-capped navvies digging out the cornered foxes. For hours on end it seems they stand around doing nothing except for the occasional, apparently inane, tootling of the horn. The thoughts that strike me even on the second run-through are 'Why are they doing this? What pleasure can possibly be had watching grown men dig enormous holes in the ground? Where are the horsemanship and working of the hounds that are supposed to be the glories of foxhunting?'

Eventually, on each occasion, the fox was reached and apparently shot. At that moment, to a great tootling of the horn and whooping as of demented children playing Red Indians, the hounds stampeded into the hole, tore up and ate the supposedly dead fox. Each time there was a shot, a group of terrier men or huntsmen made sure they were in the way of the camera to obscure the action. Strange behaviour if you are not ashamed of your activities.

Each episode struck me as showing not entertainment or sportsmanship, but a compulsion to sacrifice a fox at all cost. Perhaps that is simply it. My overall impression did not change: 'What a boring, tedious way to spend a day, and if there wasn't an animal giving its life for the entertainment the whole spectacle would be laughable.'

Take the subject up with any supporter of hunting and they will tell you that 'the fox has to be controlled'. This is not the case. If it were then why is the most heinous crime in foxhunting circles that of vulpicide – killing a fox without hunting it first? And why are hunters and gamekeepers often at loggerheads with each other?

There is another hunting myth which huntsmen use to justify their existence – that shooting is more cruel than hunting with hounds, and that many shot foxes crawl off to die of infection and gangrene from their wounds. I must say that of all the injured foxes I have rescued and treated over the years, not one was suffering from the after-effects of gunshot wounds – perhaps another hunting fallacy sunk without trace, although even I must admit that it could possibly happen. But then, I vehemently disagree with shooting as well.

Snares

When I do get a fox, or a badger, or a deer, brought in that is suffering from infection and gangrene, often that legal instrument of indiscriminate torture, the snare, has caused the injury.

A particularly graphic account of a snaring incident was splashed all over the Mail on Sunday newspaper in June 1990. Perhaps for the first time the British public were made to realise that gamekeepers and others still used snares as a method of catching wild animals. It is illegal to use snares for catching domestic animals so presumably

A fox trapped by a snare on top of a badger set

that anomaly in the law, the Protection of Animals Act 1911, which believes that domestic animals alone suffer pain whereas wild animals don't, still applies.

There are some rules and regulations concerning snares; in particular, the use of a self-locking snare is prohibited – but every animal, fox, badger, deer, or cat, that I have found in a snare has been struggling so much that even the legal, free-running snare has frayed and locked tight. The snare featured in the *Mail on Sunday* was on a fox cub and had not been checked within twenty-four hours, as legally required. Can you imagine having a steel wire noose tight around your neck, your chest, or your thighs for five minutes, let alone twenty-four hours? The pain and fear these animals suffer must be excruciating and as the animal seldom dies, the torture continues until the fiend that set the snare comes along and kills the suffering animal, usually much later than the twenty-four hours required by law. If you are a badger or deer the snare will usually be cut free from its anchor, leaving you to struggle off and die elsewhere.

I was a little concerned to read in the newspaper article that the fox was released from the snare and allowed to go

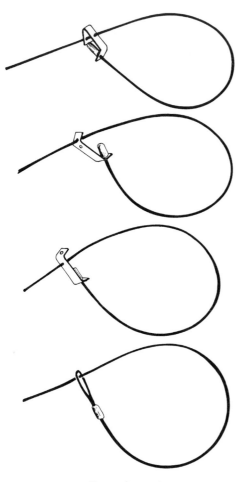

Types of snare from top to bottom; *Self-locking (illegal), dual purpose as self-locking, dual purpose as free-running and free running*

free without any medical treatment. I had a very similar experience where I was called to a fox cub in a snare. It looked to have suffered no ill effects from its garrotting but I took it back to the Hospital just to be safe. And sure enough, two days later, a line of infection erupted exactly where the wire had wound around its chest. The circular wound that appeared from nowhere took a long time to heal. Because of this I now try to stress that any animal rescued from a snare should not be released until it has been confined and observed for at least five days.

It can be very dangerous to try to release a fox, badger or any other animal from a snare. The trapped animal will be suffering the most horrific pain. It will be terrified and it will undoubtedly bite, given half the chance. But it has to be rescued or it will be killed.

The first piece of equipment you need to find, and I know this may sound ridiculous in the middle of nowhere, is some sort of strong container: a sack, a dustbin, or a large bag. Using a belt, a piece of rope, or a strong dog lead, fashion a noose that you can slip around the animal's neck to control it. I know that this sounds like further tor-ture but I would not recommend that any inexperienced person tries to scruff a wild animal (the preferred handling technique). At all times be prepared for the animal to bite. Give it the benefit of the doubt. It is faster than you, so concentrate at all times.

Once you have some control over the animal, release the snare from the anchor point, usually a staple in a log or fence post. If you regularly walk the country a good pair of fencing pliers is the only tool that will cut through snare wire. Then, lifting the animal carefully by your lead (unfortunately there is no alternative), guide it into the container and securely close it, making sure of course that the animal can breathe. Then it can be taken to a wildlife rescue centre or to a vet, where it can be sedated and the snare removed in its entirety.

If the snare was an illegal self-locking snare, you should return with a policeman or an RSPCA inspector who should then prosecute the landowner irrespective of who set the snare. The League Against Cruel Sports is running a campaign to have all snaring banned so any photographs or details of any incidents should be forwarded to their offices in London (see Useful Addresses, p. 168).

In the next chapter I will set out positive steps that can be taken to help the fox in its struggle to survive.

CHAPTER SIX

CASUALTY

Good Samaritans

It's so easy to become depressed and despondent with all these tales of cruelty to foxes and abuse of wildlife, but this torture is thankfully just the result of the libido of a few fanatics. On the whole most people would never dream of intentionally harming any animal but rather show the innate compassion, especially to injured creatures, that sets humans apart from the rest of the animal kingdom. I am particularly fortunate in that most people I meet have taken their compassion one stage further and have stopped to offer assistance to a wild animal or have made the journey to bring a casualty to the Hospital.

Just recently a vixen and two cubs ran into the path of a train on the line between Banbury and Bicester, about twenty miles from the Hospital. Breaking all the rules the distraught train driver stopped his locomotive and found one of the cubs still alive but unconscious. Keeping it warm in his cab he sped as fast as he could to the next manned station on the line, High Wycombe. Without hesitation a member of the station staff was immediately detailed to drive the cub, who became known as Casey, to us at the Hospital. It was two o'clock in the morning so the roads were clear and the mercy mission reached us about twenty minutes later.

Casey the cub was heavily con-cussed but given the right first aid of intravenous fluids to help him over the shock, and treatment with corticosteroids both to help with the shock and to reduce the inevitable inflammation caused by the collision with the train, he soon started to show signs of wak-ing up. He was a very lucky fox to have survived such an accident and soon showed the true fox forte of survival by tucking into a

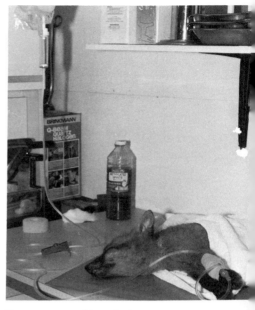

Casey, concussed by a train and rescued by its driver

bowl of Ensure (a liquid nutritional food), throwing the bowl around his cage and then promptly devouring the plastic tubing through which had flowed those initially crucial, life-giving intravenous fluids. I then had to remove the last vestiges of the first-aid tubes, still attached to his foreleg, while at the same time avoiding the snappy bites that showed he was really feeling better.

Casey was unconscious during the ordeal of the journey to the Hospital but other fox casualties being brought to us by car are regularly brought in wide awake; inexplicably they seldom cause any problem to their ambulance drivers. Somehow, something seems to protect these Samaritans who have stopped to pick up an injured ani-mal and it's not until the patient has been passed into my care that it reverts to normal, and protects itself, quite unnecessarily, I might add, by attempting to bite.

There have been so many occasions where conscious foxes and deer have been carried unrestrained inside the car that it's a wonder to me that there haven't been any serious accidents. One typical incident, I remember, happened on a particularly wet September night. One of those nights when you pull the curtains, turn on the television and do not go out unless you really have to.

But somebody had been out and about and just before midnight the door buzzer, a horrendous noise at the best of times, was pressed so urgently that it nearly flew off the wall. It had been a long day so I unlatched the front door blearily to meet a very distraught young lady who was in tears and who spluttered, 'We've got a fox!'

Her car was parked crazily across the corner of the road with lights blazing and engine racing, a sure way to upset my neighbours. I ran with her to the car and approached the boot with my usual warning, 'Don't open the boot until I have checked — ' I was stopped mid-sentence as she pulled me around to the side of the car.

'It's not in the boot, Hannah's got hold of it,' she told me agitatedly.

I fully expected a dead fox or at least one that was unconscious, but as I slowly opened the rear passenger door to meet Hannah, I could see the fox, a large one, lying across her lap with a sweater or blanket laid over it. Its eyes were closed, not as I had thought in trauma, but apparently in sheer ecstasy as Hannah fondled and stroked its ears.

I do not know if it was the sight of my bleary face or the blast of cold air as I silently opened the door but in an instant that fox had reverted to normal and was up and almost out of the blanket before I reacted. I managed to grab its scruff before it bit me or Hannah in its panic to escape.

I had broken all my own safety rules by grabbing the fox without first holding its head with a stick and Hannah had broken all the rules of common sense by cuddling a wild fox, but somehow we both got away with it. But then the only Samaritan I have ever seen injured in this situation was a woman bitten by a weasel, which escaped the moment she opened the car door in our driveway. I do not think the amnesty that the other animals observed while being taken into care can be explained, and I am convinced it is not that the animals know they are being looked after.

I am very aware of the dangers that arise when inexperienced people handle wild animals, and so whenever we receive a call about, say, an injured fox, or a deer, we instantly dispatch our 'heavy rescue' team and recommend that the callers just watch and wait until we arrive.

Drivers are very good about stopping for road casualty victims but are also often foolhardy, and I feel that groups like St Tiggywinkles should back a driver's obvious concern with urgent and positive action to assist both the animal and the finder who will also be both distraught and in need of assistance. The chart on p.96 outlines what to do.

In spite of the apparent carnage any driver might see on a journey, I am certain that any live casualty will soon be reported to the police, who will call us – that is, in this country. A short while ago a group of American students decided to conduct a research project on drivers' attitudes to road casualty animals on one of the busier roads in the

Safe procedures on finding a fox injured on the road

If you spot a fox lying on the side of the road or are unlucky enough to hit one, then pull up, either so that you are protecting it with your car, or else well away from it so that other drivers have the chance to avoid both it and you. Use your hazard warning lights to warn other drivers.

Taking particular care with other traffic, try to approach the animal from the other side of the road so that if it can and does flee it will run to the edge of the road and not onto the carriageway.

You should be able to see if the fox is still breathing by the rise and fall of its chest. If it isn't, find a large stick and hold its muzzle to the ground while you feel under its left front leg for a pulse. If there are no signs of life then please put the animal in the hedge or roadside cover, to revert to the environment. On no account try mouth-to-mouth resuscitation – it will not work and you could be endangering yourself.

If the fox is still alive then you can take one of two courses of action:

1. Using a stick you can push the fox off the carriageway, cover it with an old coat or rug to keep it warm and then summon help.

2. Once again using the stick, hold the fox's muzzle to the ground, then reach just behind its ears, firmly grasp a good scruff of skin and lift, at the same time lifting its rump by another handful of skin, just above the tail. The fox may bite, so keep well clear of its muzzle. Then place the fox flat in the boot of your car, hold its muzzle, once more with a stick, before letting go of the scruff and cover it with an old coat or rug. Then drive it to a wildlife rescue centre, or, alternatively, to a sympathetic vet.

At all times be aware that the fox may have serious injuries and be suffering intense pain, so handle it very gently and keep it as flat as possible, using a board as a stretcher if one is available.

United States. Using a stuffed possum as the victim they laid it on the carriageway and hid to see drivers' reactions. Some simply swerved to avoid it and drove on. Some showed no reaction and drove straight over the victim while a few travelling in the opposite direction actually crossed the carriageway to make sure of hitting it. But in spite of these attitudes there were many who actually stopped to see if the animal was still alive, though this included one Highway Patrol policeman who stopped, got out of his car and shot the possum!

The attitude of those swerving to avoid the casualty is encouraging, but I wish that more people had stopped to see if help was needed. The fact that the animal was stationary offered it some protection as drivers were able to avoid it. We see this in Britain where the hedgehog that curls up and sits in front of an approaching car is usually safe, whereas the hedgehog that runs gives the driver less chance of avoiding it. Foxes never sit to face oncoming traffic, preferring to use their speed to escape danger. Despite this tactic, some of them do get hit, with either fatal, or at least serious consequences.

I firmly believe that most incidents of collision with live animals are unavoidable. Most of the accidents involving large animals happen at night when the victim materialises in an instant from the gloom of the roadside, giving the driver no chance of stopping. Mind you, there used to be a television campaign that stressed: 'Drive within your headlights.' I think that if a few more adopted this code of safety then it might reduce the number of accidents by slowing vehicles enough that they could pull up in time.

Back to Hannah's fox which I held firmly in my grasp as it thrashed about trying both to escape and to take a chunk out of me. He was a very large handsome fox with not a blemish on his fine coat and thick brush. I had quite a job holding him and I think the two women suddenly realised how lucky they were not to get injured by the 'beautiful animal'.

In my struggles I made a mental note that one of his eyes was slowly closing as the skin around it swelled up. Everything else, including his four legs and definitely his jaws, seemed to have escaped injury, so it was reasonably safe for me to assume that he had been hit on the head and slightly concussed in the accident, possibly the reason why he had been so quiet during the car journey.

Deftly, or should I say desperately, I tried to lower him into my waiting carrying box but he had different ideas, spread his hind legs and slammed them across the open top, preventing me from lowering him any further. I lifted him clear and started again as he bucked and kicked, seeming to get stronger by the minute as my fingers started to ache and my grip to weaken. Eventually I managed to wiggle him inside the box and slam the lid shut at the same time as I released my grip on his scruff. He was fast and I felt the ominous touch of his snout on my retreating hand as he turned like a flash to try just one more snapping bite. But once more I got away with my fingers intact.

I know people who regularly get bitten by animals in their care and I believe they are making one great mistake. They assume that they can handle a fox without taking the precaution of using a stick or grasper to hold the animal first, or else wearing thick gloves to allay any damage if the fox does get through. Time and time again I tell people that in every situation a fit fox's reactions are infinitely faster than a human's and it will always get the better of any close encounter. But still there are those who think they are faster, and invariably they continue to get bitten.

Hannah's fox, whom I called Jaws 2 (Jaws 1 was a hedgehog who bit everyone), appeared to have survived his accident with only minor injury. He needed minimal treatment with corticosteroids and antibiotics and a few days under observation before being released where he had been found, hopefully this time with a bit more learned road sense.

The foxes I have mentioned so far, Casey and Jaws 2, both escaped with minor concussive injuries that required just a modicum of medical attention, but some obviously suffer far more serious injuries and then can amaze us all with their phenomenal powers of recovery.

Treating fox casualties

A human being who has been the victim of a road accident will receive the latest in sophisticated treatments, first to save his or her life, then to relieve pain, and then to treat any injuries, no matter how serious or hopeless they may seem.

Except in the most extenuating of circumstances I believe that any injured animal, especially a fox, should always receive the best treatment available. The extenuating circumstances where euthanasia would be the only answer would be confirmed severe injuries such as a broken back, the loss of two or more legs, irreparable jaw or head damage, or some condition in which there is absolutely no chance of recovery. But in all cases I would insist that only a veterinary surgeon should make that decision and even then only after serious consideration of possible alternatives.

Although I have mentioned euthanasia at this point, I would like to see outlawed the present form of words: 'putting an animal out of its misery'. Euthanasia is a very humane-sounding word but it does mean killing, the extinction of life, and should be resorted to only if there is no other viable alternative. To my mind killing can never be a sound first-aid measure, only a last resort.

Most injured animals show a remarkable lack of pain response, although pain must be present and can be eased with painkillers. Handling them quietly and gently helps alleviate distress and gives the animal-handlers, and the vets, time to make a prognosis and either treat the animal or kill it. My experience has been that few injured wild animals are beyond saving and although at the Hospital we deal with over 10,000 casualties of all species every year, only a handful have to be referred to the vets for destruction.

The killing itself should be carried out by an injection into a vein. The procedure is painless and instant, the unfortunate animal just seems to drop off to sleep. Never, ever allow the injection to be given anywhere other than into a vein unless the animal is anaesthetised first. Injections to the heart, liver, or other organs can be very, very painful and should be resisted.

An animal will do all in its power to live, no matter what the circumstances. I feel we owe it to animals to use our knowledge to give them any chance to survive.

So let's get on with the business of trying to save lives. There are methods available to anybody dealing with animal casualties and they should be used as incidents arise.

Let me describe a typical incident, one in which I was recently involved. I was called to an injured fox that had

My heart sank when I saw a three-legged fox, with one leg broken

been hit by a car in Amersham, about fifteen miles from Aylesbury. We always pride ourselves that our 'heavy rescue' teams can be on the road instantly, when called to a fox or a badger, a heron or a swan.

I left immediately and in the high-powered, fourwheel-drive Land Cruiser, part of a small fleet loaned to us by Toyota, I was able to be at the scene in fifteen minutes. The fox, it looked like a small vixen, had hobbled down a bank and was lying against the wall of a house. I carry a large net for these situations and as I approached, crouched down so as not to appear too large, the fox tried to move off. My heart sank: the fox appeared to have only three legs, and one of those was obviously broken.

(Seen from a distance a broken leg looks loose and because the animal cannot control it the limb tends to hang uselessly. If an animal is limping but still using an injured leg, it may only have a sprain or torn muscle and can sometimes recover without any intervention.)

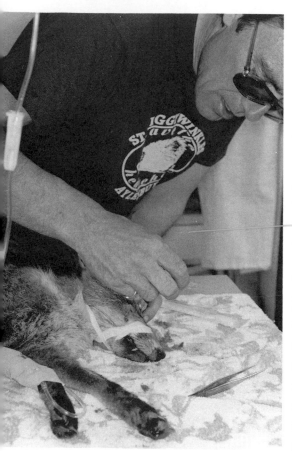

I always muzzle a casualty

The vixen could not move very fast but there was still a danger that if she escaped my approach she could drag herself through a hole in a nearby hedge, straight into the main carriageway of the Amersham to Rickmansworth road. I could feel every painful step she tried to take, only ever managing to drag her broken leg behind her. I had to catch her quickly to ease her agony so, without hesitation, I dived between her and the hedge and had her in my net and unable to move. Carefully, I held her still while I extricated the net and temporarily strapped the broken leg to a splint to ease her inevitable pain. Doing this single-handed was not easy but I soon had her settled and restricted in a carrying basket for the journey to the Hospital where I could make a more comprehensive assessment of her condition and injuries.

I was back in Aylesbury after another fifteen minutes' hair-raising driving and could get a good look at the little vixen as I weighed her in the carrying basket. There was no sign of a wound where her other hind leg had been so it seemed that she had managed very well on three legs until that fateful day when she fractured one of these, probably in an encounter with a car on that busy Amersham to Rickmansworth road.

The little fox, she weighed only 4.9 kilograms, was very stressed and in typical fear defecated and urinated as I lifted her from the carrying basket. In this situation we often administer a safe, short-acting sedative that will relax the animal, making it easier to approach. An anaesthetic of any form could be dangerous to a shocked animal so should be avoided for at least twenty-four hours, or until the casualty is stable.

I know diazepam has had a mixed reception in human circles, but in animals it has proven to be a very safe, short-acting sedative that allows many stressed animals to be treated without the added trauma of their having to be restrained physically. However, even when an animal has been given diazepam, or when an injured fox or badger is naturally unconscious, I will always muzzle the casualty with a five-centimetre cotton bandage, just to be on the safe side.

The dose rate for diazepam is approximately 1.0 mg/kg given by intravenous or intramuscular injection. This little vixen, whom we named Barbie, was given hers into the muscle of her remaining back leg, well above the site of the obvious fracture. She was muzzled and was relaxing even as we laid her on a warmed pad to start treating her for shock.

Shock, in its medical sense, both in animals and humans, is a serious physiological change that if uncorrected can lead to a self-perpetuating, downward spiral into death. Very, very simply the cardiovascular system normally sends its life-giving blood to the extremes of the body and removes waste products generated by the body cells. In shock the extremes of the body are deprived of this circulating blood in the peripheral tissues, the waste products accumulate, and the net result of this, coupled with the lack of oxygen and nutrients, is cellular death. A shocked patient feels cold to the touch as the finer blood capillaries in the skin and limbs close down. Gentle warmth is the first course of action to keep those capillaries open. So we covered Barbie and placed her on a warmed heat pad, even before more radical assistance could be given. However, too much heat could have resulted in a disastrous lowering of her blood pressure, a condition we had to avoid.

She was by then warm and quiet and lying on our operating table. She looked so tiny and, even sedated as she was, you could almost sense the pain and stress her little body had gone through since the fracturing of her leg. Gently I lifted her front leg and shaved some of the thick fur between her wrist and elbow, allowing an intravenous catheter to be inserted and attached to a drip, so that fluids could be given to save her life.

By the time we had completed all our life-saving procedures, and given Barbie a plasma expander (to ease the effects of shock), steroids, pain-relieving drugs and an antibiotic, she was warm and comfortable. All that was then required was to re-strap the broken leg in a more sophisticated manner until the vet decided which form of remedial treatment would be taken once the little fox had recovered enough to be anaesthetised.

We temporarily stabilise any leg fractures with a very simplified version of a Robert Jones bandage which, in

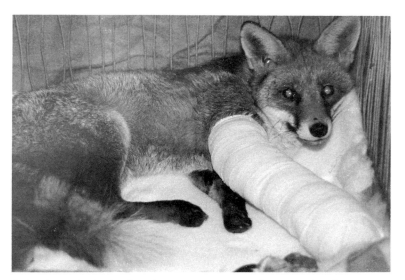

A dog fox with a broken front leg in an enormous 'Robert Jones' bandage

effect, encases the fracture site in a cocoon of cotton wool and stabilises the fractured bones. First, we clean any breaks in the skin with dilute Hibiscrub (a safe disinfectant) and generally line up the fracture in the right direction (reduce). Any wounds are then covered with sterile non-adhesive dressings (Melolin) held loosely in place with five-centimetre Elastoplast tape. The whole leg is then wrapped in one layer of cotton wool. A splint (plastic, wood, or aluminium) is laid along the leg and the whole thing is wrapped in seven or eight layers of cotton wool. This is then covered with a tight wrapping of conforming bandage, ten to fifteen centimetres wide. Finally, the whole is then covered tightly with self-adhesive bandage, Co-form, which is what most vets will have in stock.

Once we had wrapped Barbie's broken leg she was laid in a recovery cage on a Vet-Bed, which is like a lamb's-wool rug that allows any fluid or urine to pass through.

Caring for a sick fox

1. You will need a strong indoor metal pen or a secure indoor aviary with at least 12-gauge wire mesh set on a concrete base; a sick fox will dig its way out of anything on a soil or sand base, and will eat through wooden bars.

2. Offer a debilitated fox rehydrating fluid instead of water. Lectade, made by SmithKline Beecham, is readily available from vets; you can if necessary make up your own (but only, please, as a stop-gap measure) by mixing:

   1 tablespoon of sugar
   1 teaspoon of salt
   1 quart (1.1 litres) warm water
   (Use within twenty-four hours)

3. If the fox appears very undernourished, offer it one of the liquid diets available from chemists. Try to get a product called Ensure if you can; if not, use Complan.

4. After twenty-four hours on a liquid diet, if the fox seems capable of taking solid food, offer it a bowl of Pedigree Chum Puppy Food sprinkled with one of the veterinary supplements, either Vet-a-min plus zinc or SA37.

5. After a day or two of dog food, wean the fox onto a more

Using these keeps any recumbent animal dry and clean until it can stand up and look after itself. There was an overhead infra-red heater to keep her warm and quiet for at least twenty-four hours or until the vet thought her strong enough for further examination and possible treatment to her broken leg.

Any wild animal casualty picked up and brought to the Hospital will be suffering from some degree of shock. The road traffic victim found at the scene of the accident will natural diet. Carnivores do not just eat meat, they eat whole animals, and without the proper diet they will soon be short of essential nutrients. Various suppliers sell frozen day-old chicks, a by-product of the massive chicken industry, from factory hatching units where millions of chickens are hatched every year. Foxes will readily take this food, which can be given extra nutritional value by a once-weekly sprinkling with one of the multi-vitamin preparations.

6. A fox which has suffered fractures benefits if Pet-Cal Tablets (available from the vet) are added to its food, supplying a calcium and vitamin D supplement.

7. Captive foxes will also eat chicken heads (discarded by butchers) and fresh road kills of rabbits or mice.

8. Foxes must have water available at all times. They seem to take great delight in tipping bowls over but a heavy ceramic dish might just be beyond their powers of mischief.

9. Most foxes in for treatment will have lost weight and muscle mass. To build up their strength give them a daily dose of anabolic steroids in tablet form, hidden in their food; just one 5mg Nandoral tablet a day while the fox is in captivity, will give it a much better chance when it is returned to the wild.

generally have good body condition to help it recover. However, many fox casualties have old, long-standing injuries or problems like mange and are not found and caught until infection or a blend of starvation, exhaustion and dehydration has finally brought them down. An animal in this condition will appear very thin and small; its skin will be dry or crusted in the case of mange; its eyes will appear sunken and it will be generally too weak to put up even a token resistance to capture. A fox in this condition is in severe shock and on the point of dying.

The routine shock treatment of intravenous therapy must be instigated immediately. Analgesics are probably not necessary but the drug Flunixin meglumine is essential for its anti-inflammatory and anti-toxaemia qualities.

Treatment of the underlying conditions can start once the intravenous therapy is dripping in. Any fox in poor condition and without the surefire symptoms of mange is going to be suffering from some form of infection, which may not necessarily be disease. Bite wounds, fractures, snare wounds and, apparently, shot wounds, can all become infected enough to bring the fox down. Initially a course of broad-spectrum antibiotic like amoxycillin could be started but bacterial swabs should be taken at the infection site so that a sensitivity test will indicate a specific antibiotic.

Every precaution should be taken just in case the fox is suffering from a disease that is transferable to humans. A vet will make the ultimate diagnosis and prescribe a suitable remedy.

Once you have an injured or sick fox in captivity then it is necessary to house it properly and offer a good balanced diet, as described in the chart on p. 106–7.

In this chapter I have highlighted the few common instances that crop up time and time again. The prime object is to save the fox's life and then to follow up the success with more extended treatments and rehabilitation in order to return the fox to its wild existence. First and crucially the rescuer gives the animal first aid; then, after the vet has prescribed a course of treatment, comes the tending, feeding and cleaning of the convalescent until that ultimate goal of releasing a fit-again fox.

There is just one golden rule that must be remembered when you are close to any fox – that the fox is at all times terrified of you and will always bite, given the opportunity. So never take a fox for granted, it is behaving in the only way it knows. Should you get even a scratch from a fox's teeth then refer yourself to your local hospital for anti-tetanus and antibiotic medication.

Some simple treatments may be all that is necessary with a fox but there may be more serious injuries and sophisticated problems that can only be dealt with by anaesthetising the animal. This is the vet's domain and can mean all the difference between a fox fit for release and one that has to spend the rest of its life in captivity.

The general rule with fox casualties of all ages is not to let the fox become too friendly, or it may never be wild enough for release.

CHAPTER SEVEN

INTENSIVE CARE

Barbie

At our house in Aylesbury, where we ran the Wildlife Hospital for so many years, all our large casualties were housed in a new shed fitted with six special stainless steel cages. Barbie was housed in one of the top two cages so that we could monitor how the intravenous drip was running and generally keep an eye on her condition.

We need not have worried, for in true fox tradition as soon as she felt better she bit through her intravenous drip, scattering fluids all over the floor and on the badger in the cage below hers.

Not to be beaten, I managed to attach a new drip without her biting me and just to thwart her I fitted one of those plastic Elizabethan collars that are used on dogs, to stop her attacking the new plastic tubing. She must have thought this was a new game for no sooner had I left the shed than she ripped the collar off, chewed and tore at it so that it was unusable, and then started on the drip again – beheading it and splattering another bag of fluids over the floor of the cage and the unfortunate badger.

Four times I renewed her drip that night but gave up in

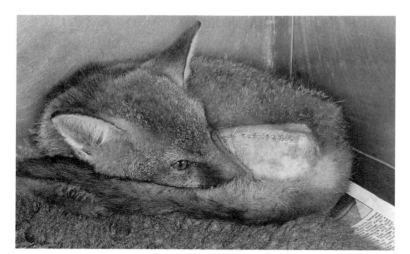

Barbie's smart row of stitches

the end after assessing that in spite of her shenanigans I had managed to get enough fluid into her to stabilise her condition and prepare her for more intense treatments on her broken leg.

Obviously in our back garden set-up we had no x-ray facilities or the antiseptic conditions necessary for a vet to operate on Barbie's broken leg. We had to rely on local veterinary practices doing our surgical work even though it was tremendously expensive, especially to carry out an operation on a broken leg that needed either a stainless steel pin inserted down the centre of the broken bone, or a plate screwed on to hold the fracture together.

Barbie had broken her femur, the main bone in her leg, and when she was x-rayed the vets decided that a stainless steel plate was the answer and so carried out the operation. They generally keep a patient in for twenty-four hours' observation; as the operation went well, we were able to pick Barbie up the following day.

She looked forlorn and damp and was sore where all the fur had been shaved off her rump and her back leg around the operation site. But instead of the bulky Robert Jones bandage restricting her broken leg, she now had just a smart line of stitches where the plate had been inserted. And, best of all, she had some use in the leg which, although a trifle stiff, did enable her to move and allow her to keep herself clean. Cleanliness is of paramount importance to any fox, especially Barbie who started to look so much better once she had managed to groom herself. Mind you, she did look a little strange with her hindquarters shaved, and parts of her front legs shaved too where the drips had been inserted. We would have to let all the fur grow back before we could envisage releasing her, or she might suffer during cold or wet weather.

Amazingly, after a few days of good food and antibiotics, coupled with safe anabolic steroids to build her weight up, she was completely mobile on her three legs, although the hind leg was still a bit stiff. After ten days, when we took her stitches out, the leg seemed very firm.

Dental treatment

Over the ten days of her treatment Barbie had tried to bite me every time I moved her, and I had noticed that at least one of her main canine teeth was broken and that the pulp cavity inside was exposed. This type of dental injury was probably causing her discomfort but, more ominously, there was a danger of infection getting into the cavity, which could lead to gum disease and further complications that might eventually and painfully lead to her death. Barbie needed a visit to the dentist.

This was not as easy as it sounds. Human teeth are soft,

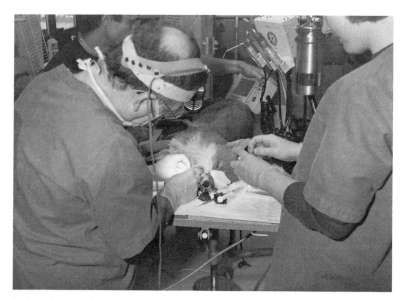

A dental surgery in operation

small and shallow-rooted and so dental equipment designed for use on humans generally cannot cope with animal teeth, especially those that are the armoury of carnivores. Local veterinary practices usually have only equipment for cleaning teeth and extracting diseased ones. I did not want Barbie to lose her teeth unnecessarily as they were the means of her survival in the wild. However, I knew of one dentist who specialised in animal dental work: Peter Kertesz. His equipment was strong enough to cope with the size and hardness of animal teeth and he could give Barbie a complete overhaul, including root-filling the badly damaged tooth, though he will never carry out cosmetic work, such as crowns and caps, on animals' teeth as these could never be strong enough to withstand the wear and tear of an animal's lifestyle.

Peter was booked in to visit and overhaul Barbie's teeth.

The whole operation could take some hours so at the same time we had to arrange for our consultant vet, Dr John Lewis of the International Zoo Veterinary Group, to handle the sophisticated anaesthetic Barbie would need to receive.

Peter and Sam, his nurse, set up a complete dental surgery in our little shed. There were strong lights, drills, suction equipment and all those horrible instruments we dread on our visits to our own dentist.

The whizz of the drill and the smell of burning enamel wafted around the improvised surgery. And the little pieces of wire twisted in root cavities brought back such memories of my own dental ordeals. But it was all worth it: Peter did not have to remove a single tooth, even though he had to drill and fill at least two of her canines and two teeth further back in her mouth.

During all of this Barbie was blissfully unaware, asleep under John's anaesthetic. She was woken up later and given painkillers for a couple of days to eliminate any discomfort. She probably felt much better because she had no cavities to give her gyp every time she ate anything.

Following on from Peter's visit we now insist that before it is released every animal has its teeth checked and, if necessary, treated. This regime is particularly important for the carnivores but can be equally essential for smaller animals like rabbits, hedgehogs and field mice.

Fractures

Barbie was fortunate that the fracture in her leg healed well. As it has been proved, time and again, that three-legged foxes live perfectly well in the wild, two months later she was released back where I had first picked her up.

As most of the animals in the Hospital have suffered from an accident of one kind or another we do see a great many fractures and, as we now have our own x-ray facilities and operating theatre at the new Hospital, we find that most of them respond well to the correct treatment.

However, we do sometimes find that a fox casualty's hind legs do not seem to work after an accident. This is a very worrying situation as the spine or pelvis may be fractured, or there may be damage to the nerves themselves. An x-ray will highlight actual fractures but if the spinal column is broken then there is no chance of recovery and the fox should be humanely destroyed.

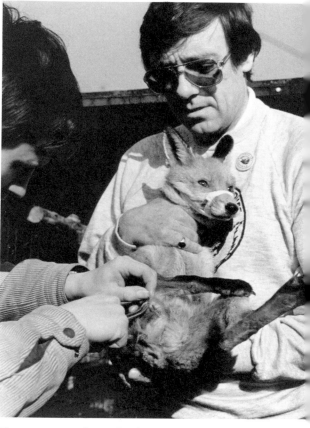

The vet removes the stitches from a casualty

A broken pelvis is another matter and this can often be allowed to heal by just confining the fox to a small cage for three to six weeks. The vet, however, may plump for some heroic orthopaedic surgery giving a more positive healing.

Fractures of the tail usually result in its having to be amputated. However, the loss of its crowning glory, its

Unable to move but receiving treatment

brush, does not seem to bother a fox. We recently had a fox at the Hospital whom we christened Bob, for obvious reasons.

Bob lived on a nearby RAF base and was spotted one day looking very sick and worn. I went out and caught him with very little effort, always a bad sign with any wild animal. When I arrived back at the Hospital, Dr John Lewis, our consultant vet, was working in our veterinary unit. So while I went through all the various life-saving shock procedures, John assessed Bob's injuries which appeared to have been caused during a run-in with a dog. Bob had apparently been injured some time before the capture, as all the bite wounds were badly infected. His tail had obviously been bitten through and was hanging from a wound, so John decided, there and then, on the minor surgery necessary to amputate the remains.

Bob had an abscess in the left shoulder which was

quickly lanced, but any treatment of this and other bite wounds on his front legs was left until the intravenous fluids had had a chance to stabilise his condition.

The following day Bob was much brighter so we could concentrate on cleaning his wounds and check suspected damage to his front ankle. The cleaning and irrigation of the wounds would not cause any pain so we were able to give Bob just one treatment of diazepam to ease the stress of being handled. His generally low condition made it inadvisable even to contemplate anaesthesia.

When dealing with an animal that has infected wounds, it can be an advantage to leave any cleaning and treatment until the fox is more stable. Jumping straight in as soon as the patient arrives can add stress to the shock it is already suffering from. Bob's wounds had been infected for some while so another twenty-four or forty-eight hours would make no difference. And anyway initial antibiotic injections would serve to hold any infection in abeyance. We will only treat wounds on an animal at the admittance stage if the wounds are fresh and need suturing, or if there are maggots present that need removing.

Eventually after many weeks with the joint strapped, Bob could manage to walk very well. He then spent a period in one of our outside pens to harden him off before he was released back to his home territory on the RAF camp.

Other orthopaedic problems are fairly common in foxes and they cope very well with these. Even if a fractured leg has to be amputated the fox will still be able to manage in its wild environment, although I might be reluctant to release a fox with a missing front leg as it would not be able to dig. Sometimes damage to hips is irreparable. A fox suffers considerable pain if the top of its femur does not sit comfortably in the acetabulum (hip socket). However, the vet can perform an operation called an excision arthroplasty, wherein the head of the femur is surgically removed. A fibrous false joint will form, allowing the fox nearly normal use of the leg, and it will certainly be good enough to function in the wild.

Difficulties in diagnosis

By far the most frustrating casualties that arrive at a rescue centre are those animals with no outward signs of injury or disease. I have just been out to Wigginton, a village near Tring in Hertfordshire, to retrieve a fox that did not run off when a dog approached it. The dog's owners had even taken bowls of dog food to the fox but it still showed no reaction whatsoever. Thank goodness there is still no rabies in Britain as this could have been a classic situation featuring an infected fox.

When I arrived the fox was standing in a field of high corn. I am sure I would have missed it completely had the dog not found it in the first place. I approached it from the rear and gently slid the loop of a grasper over its head. I had not expected it to be that easy to catch and had arrived equipped with large nets, which are the only thing to use when catching mobile foxes.

The fox, a vixen, offered no resistance whatsoever so I scruffed her neck and released the grasper. Putting her into a carrying box I took a perfunctory look to see if there were any injuries and any traces of mange. Generally when a fox is that weak and approachable it is in the advanced stages of sarcoptic mange but this vixen had a very good coat. There was a group of fly eggs on one side but still nothing to suggest any injury.

Back at the Hospital, we donned surgical gloves before handling the fox, just in case. We carried out standard shock procedures, setting up an intravenous drip and infusing suitable drugs. Even though the fox was very subdued, we still muzzled her with a ten-centimetre cotton bandage. We also fitted a plastic Elizabethan collar, to prevent her getting at the infusion line, at least for the time being. Or so we hoped.

There were no outward signs of injury so we could only assume that some type of disease had dragged the fox down. The field where she had been found was well away from any roads, so it was unlikely that her subdued state was caused by concussion, but I suppose poisoning could have been a possibility. As it was, we took no chances and after giving her an antibiotic injection, settled her into a warm cage to await diagnostic tests at the vet's next visit. Strict hygiene was observed at all times just in case her problem was a zoonosis (an infection that could be passed on to humans).

When I looked at her next she seemed brighter but was visibly panting. As I opened her cage door to check the drip, she seemed to go into spasms and then she died. I still do not know what had been wrong with her but I have instructed the vet to carry out a full post-mortem examination. It will not help this fox but it might give us some ideas if another sick fox arrives without obvious injuries.

I suppose that if there had been a snare involved it could have left its legacy by way of unseen compression injuries. This does often happen. Some days after a snare has been removed, the cells which were injured by the pressure break down and erupt as a circle of necrosis and resultant infection following the original line of the wire. We now keep a look-out for this in snare cases and then treat the wounds with Dermisol Multicleanse Solution (SmithKline Beecham) followed by applications of Intra-Site (Smith & Nephew) every second day. Both these products enhance the healing of infected wounds, with the IntraSite producing the nice, moist environment that wounds need to encourage them to heal.

A snare may also be wrapped around a fox's leg, efficiently cutting into the skin as the fox struggles to escape and eventually cutting off the blood supply – which can lead to gangrene and the loss of the leg. A similar situation may arise if a fox catches its legs on a wire fence as it tries to leap over. The wire ligature in both cases can cut bone-deep, exposing muscle, ligament and bone to infection. We dress the leg with a veterinary product called BioDres, which, like IntraSite, produces the moist environment that encourages wounds to heal. If the paw and the limb below the wound feel warm, then you can usually save the leg, but if they feel cold and hard the animal may have to be referred to the vet for possible amputation. But as I have said before, foxes cope very well on three good legs.

In all cases foxes are similar to dogs so it should be possible for the veterinary surgeon to investigate, diagnose and, if practicable, treat almost any condition which may arise.

Whenever a fox arrives at the Hospital it's my job to assess its condition, stabilise it and cope with any wounds or injuries. Obviously if I learn the circumstances of its rescue then I have a good idea of what its injuries are going to be. The real conundrum occurs when there is no history of an accident or when there is nothing obviously wrong.

Then even the vets sometimes have great difficulty diag-
nosing just what is wrong with the fox, and of course in
subsequently setting up a course of treatment.

One of the problems has been that until the advent of
wildlife care over the last few years very few people had
previously bothered about treating a sick fox and the pro-
hibitive cost of laboratory diagnosis and identification of
disease means that very little serious investigation was
done and almost no treatment was even contemplated.

Thankfully wildlife in general has more or less mastered
diseases with natural immunity and the fittest animals survive while the weaker, diseased animals die before they
can reproduce. Every so often an epizootic (an epidemic in
animals) will sweep through a specific wild population,
especially if the numbers of that species are unusually
high. The epizootic will run its course without necessarily
affecting another species, while any survivors (there are
always some) will have acquired a degree of immunity and
can prosper.

At the Wildlife Hospital we see very little evidence of
diseases debilitating foxes, except perhaps the one scourge
that seems to have been blighting southern British populations for at least the last five years: sometimes incorrectly
labelled 'fox' mange, it is in fact sarcoptic mange, which
makes some vets panic a little bit as it can be a serious
problem to cure in dogs, though it is comparatively easy to
treat in foxes.

Mange
Mange in foxes is caused by mites. The two species of mite
involved are both minute members of the spider family,
the *Arachnidae*. Only really visible through a microscope,

these two species, *Sarcoptes scabiei* and *Notoedres notoedres*, burrow into the layers of skin, forming a scab of dried fluid. The hair falls out and the dead skin cells typically form a horrible crust over the whole area of the body affected. The infestation usually starts on the rump and tail, gradually spreading along the body onto the head and round the eyes. There is also sometimes secondary infection invading the damaged skin.

The mange gradually saps the strength of the fox by constant irritation which prevents the animal from resting or sleeping. The fox slowly succumbs to exhaustion. Unable to hunt, it loses weight until eventually it collapses and dies. For some reason many foxes seem to make for human habitation just when they are on their last legs, hiding themselves away in a barn or outhouse. A more pitiful sight than an animal dying of mange I cannot imagine – the fox which once had such a fine coat is now hairless with a thick, cracked crust of dead skin, it is terribly thin and shrunken, and all its discomfort shows in its sunken, encrusted eyes. Although it may still be able to move, a fox suffering from mange can quickly be overhauled and caught.

One that I rescued at High Wycombe had found its way under an up-and-over garage door in the middle of a housing estate. Inside the garage he had ripped up an old mattress as bedding and was lying curled up in abject misery.

I quietly rolled myself under the up-and-over and pulled it closed after me. Quite unlike a fox he took some time to realise I was there, but slowly, painfully, he opened his crusted eyes and in a flash of adrenalin, perhaps his last, bolted under a workbench. In the open I would have had to struggle even with a fox as dejected as this one, but in

A dramatic recovery from mange

this enclosed area I soon secured him with my grasper and got him into a carrying basket.

He was no larger than a cub, but from his eyes and teeth I could tell he was an adult, a once proud dog fox who had wasted away because the mange mites had exhausted him, making it more and more difficult to hunt. Perhaps that is why he had chosen to spend his last days on a housing estate, where he could scavenge for rubbish and scraps.

As the fox looked at me from the carrying basket, he was all head and ears, his body wasted to just skin and bone. He seemed resigned to dying there and then as his sore eyes closed and he curled in the bottom of the basket, with his bare stalk of a tail curled over him in a futile attempt at keeping warm.

This is one of the few instances where we at the Hospital interfere with nature. Some 95 per cent of our casualties need treatment as a result of their encounters with the artificial human environment. The remainder are probably suffering from natural occurrences and the old adage 'Let nature take its course' is often thrown at our efforts. I, for one, cannot pass by any animal that needs help, and a fox suffering from mange looks so miserable and desperate that I will do all in my power to save it.

I know it will feel wretched and miserable for a few days, but given the chance to recover, it will be up and raring to bite you in just one week, even though it will still be bald and skinny. And in six weeks' it will be ready for release, and it won't look back at the misery it has gone through.

Every now and then we witness a run of mange cases, especially after a mild winter. Mange can definitely kill a fox that does not receive treatment and there have been well-recorded epizootics where the local fox population has been reduced by up to 80 per cent. It seems localised in its effects however, and whereas we see numerous cases here in the south of England, rescue centres in central Scotland see none whatsoever.

Dogs and other animals (including hedgehogs) are all candidates for attack by mange mites but once again, in spite of the propaganda, there appears to be little risk of neighbourhood foxes spreading the infection to domestic animals.

And humans can catch mange mites, although the disease is then known as scabies. The only real risk, however, occurs if you handle foxes with mange and are terribly unlucky or careless in doing so. Once you have it, however, it takes a lot of daubing all over the body with benzyl benzoate to get rid of the problem. We treat many, many foxes that have mange but only once has one of our medical team been afflicted with full-blown scabies. However, we all seem to suffer from an allergy to mange mites which brings us out in an itching rash that takes two or three weeks to clear. We all now wear surgical gloves, masks and aprons when handling affected foxes and seem to have overcome the problem.

Taking precautions

Foxes, being of the dog family, are susceptible to canine diseases such as canine distemper, canine parvovirus and infectious canine hepatitis, and the fact that these have not been recorded in British wildlife foxes remains something of a mystery – or a miracle. It may be because foxes go out of their way to avoid dogs, so the possibility of cross-infection from a dog is kept to a minimum. This behaviour might be of strategic importance if rabies were ever to breach our quarantine laws and invade Britain.

I do not want to deter anybody from giving a helping hand to a wildlife casualty, but I must insist that every precaution is taken to keep working areas clean and that tetanus inoculations are up-to-date. And always follow the golden rules: no drinking, no smoking, no eating around animals, and always wash, *not* scrub, your hands, after any contact whatsoever.

There is certainly no room for complacency where rabies is concerned, particularly in rabies-free Britain. But even though the fox is the main vector of rabies across the rest of Europe, it has, thankfully, been proven that this particular epizootic is far better controlled and eradicated by oral vaccines, dropped by aeroplane, than by the old shoot-everything-on-sight policy which actually encourages the spread of the virus. Should the virus break out in Britain, I am sure the use of this proven treatment should mean that foxes will not be killed indiscriminately.

CHAPTER EIGHT

YOUNG AND BOISTEROUS

The untamed spirit

Recently there have been some very successful campaigns
to curb the sale of puppies displayed in pet shop windows,
especially at Christmas. The campaigns have been made
necessary by the puppies themselves because nobody can
resist their adorable charm. Watching television, we are
constantly assailed by their cute, cuddly appeal as they
waylay us into buying toilet rolls, dog food, shoes, every
household item you can think of. Puppies are the epitome
of everything that is attractive to us, the perfect compan-
ion, the perfect pet.

Now imagine a puppy with twice as much agility, oodles
more playfulness, one as engaging as a kitten and with an
intelligence and loyalty that even Lassie would be proud
of. You are imagining a typical fox cub. But under the
chocolate-box image of the fox cub there simmers the
spirit that only a truly wild animal possesses. This is an
animal that should never be petted. Rather, its wildness,
so easy to tame and disguise, should be protected and nurtured and if you meet a fox cub face to face, you should be
thrilled at its cold courage as it snaps and snarls at you.

This is the law of the jungle that was so much a part of the wilderness that was Britain in centuries past and is sadly now disappearing.

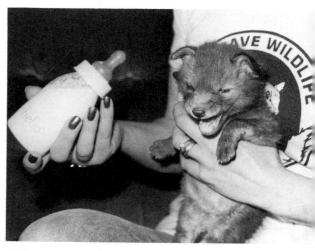

Agile, engaging and intelligent: a typical fox cub

Offer a fox cub food of any kind and it will almost rip off your hand as it takes it. If it is with its other siblings it will fight them tooth to tooth to keep its prize while they attack with similar fury. We feed our weaned fox cubs on defrosted frozen chicks and every mealtime we have to jump out of the way as each cub snatches its share, still managing to fight, snarl, yap and spit even with a mouth crammed full of seven or eight chicks. The puppy charm goes straight out of the window as the spirit of a wild animal shines through, nature in the raw, the survival of the fittest.

To me, this is one of the great privileges of working with wild animals and birds, this untamed, uninhibited spirit we see in young foxes, wild cats, sparrowhawks and even diminutive weasels and shrews, both of which will unwaveringly take on even a giant human being.

The first months of life

Yet, when it is born, the fox cub is blind, deaf and helpless. Its mother has been pregnant for seven and a half weeks and has prepared a nursery for her offspring. There is no bedding, just the bare earth, but when the young are born the vixen stays with them for two weeks, using her warm body and lush fur to keep her precious charges cosy and protected.

The babies weigh between 80 and 120 grams at birth and are covered in short, dark fur which is charcoal grey, almost black, in colour. The vixen probably gives birth to four or five cubs in a litter, each of which knows her and whimpers for attention with little 'care' calls that are so insistent and more demanding when the temperature is low and the early spring humidity high.

Most fox cubs are born between the middle of March and the middle of April; another one of nature's miracles apparently geared so that when the cubs have grown and start hunting, over six weeks later, there will be a luxuriant growth of plants in the fields and hedgerows offering a surfeit of easily caught young voles and mice – ideal prey for the young foxes' first clumsy attempts at hunting.

Fox cubs are deceptively friendly when very young

During those crucial first two weeks as the cubs suckle from the vixen, the dog fox (and sometimes the non-breeding females in the group) brings food to the mother to sustain her during her fortnight below ground. The cubs are helpless but at about two weeks they will make their first attempts to crawl, whimpering for their mother if they stray outside the circle of her warmth. Their eyes will start to open, a quite unfoxlike slate-blue in colour. Their ears are opening too. Young cubs can be taken at this age for kittens.

A devoted mother, this vixen was treated for a damaged hip and restored to her cubs at the concrete works where she had made their home

During the next week the vixen will occasionally leave her charges, who will form themselves into furry little pyramids to keep warm. They cannot thermoregulate themselves – keep their own bodies warm – for a few more days yet, and as they are starting to urinate without stimulation they can get quite damp in between the vixen's returns from her excursions. At about nineteen days their care calls change from whimpers to short sharp barks.

Three weeks of age sees the eruption of the first milk teeth and the parents begin to offer the cubs regurgitated semi-solid food. In captivity, fox cubs of this age will take minced liver and tinned puppy foods like Friskies or Pedigree Chum Puppy Food. The cubs' appearance starts to change, with the first black markings showing from eyes to the muzzle. Over the next few days the muzzle starts to elongate into the true fox shape and takes on the adult white which, with the ears starting to prick up, at last gives the image of a fox.

The cubs are now both more aware and also more agile.

They greet their parents with ears flattened, tails wagging and an excited whimpering yap. A captive fox cub will do this to its feeder. It is charming and resolve-melting but anyone rearing cubs should resist these come-ons at all costs. A tame, or imprinted, fox has no place in captivity or in the wild.

The vixen now works hard at weaning her offspring with more and more regurgitated food and fewer opportunities for suckling. She will often sleep away from the earth to encourage the cubs to cope with the softened solid food. The more dominant male cubs will grow faster as they take the lion's share of the food. Each mealtime will be accompanied by a lot of screaming and scrapping as the cubs fight for each morsel, often with the smallest cub being the most aggressive. Playing is all part of a fox's growing up and when the cubs venture out of the earth at about six weeks old, fighting will be essential for their development. It is then that they start to practise their hunting skills, perfecting the typical fox pounce for vole-catching, even at this early age.

As they come out of the earth at this time their appearance has changed yet again. Their little brown noses have turned black, as have their legs and their now pointed ears. The white patches on their upper lips gleam distinctly and an observer can easily make out the site of the supra-caudal, violet gland on the tail. The male fox cubs in a litter will have grown more than the little vixens.

If the weather is fine and there is little disturbance, young cubs will play outside during the day, but if not, they will stay below ground until dark. The vixen will usually be nearby, watching for danger, and her single short bark will send the cubs scurrying back into their earth.

A young cub will fit into the palm of your hand

Some observers believe that the litters are split into different earths at about this time and that they may even be segregated by sex. This could be understandable as it gives the smaller female cubs a better chance in the customary fights for food. Also some wild animals seem to like to spread their litters.

The cubs still attempt to suckle off their mother but those that are weaned will be sent packing to give the others a chance and the vixen a break. In the next two weeks all the cubs will attain their full complement of milk teeth and will be losing their long juvenile fur which is replaced by the typical yellow-brown hairs of the fox. They start to live above ground in close thickets and will demand up to 350 grams of food each day. Now is the time when the forward family planning pays off, with an abundance of small mammals and birds in the countryside, all experiencing their own adolescence and falling easy prey to the adult foxes. The cubs themselves will be picking up worms and insects and practising their foxy pounces, mainly on their brothers or sisters.

By the end of July they have lost all their milk teeth and

By the end of July, a cub is three-quarters grown

now have a full set of gleaming, sharp, adult teeth. They will be three-quarters grown and almost self-sufficient. But as August and September dawn the halcyon days are over and, although lighter in weight than mature foxes, they must make their own way into the future. Even if they don't get eaten by fox hounds the male cubs will sally forth to search for one of the abundant territories. Most of the female cubs will stay in the vicinity of their parents and become non-breeding vixens to help rear the following year's cubs – that is if there is a next year because few of these juvenile foxes ever see their first birthday and those that do will probably get no older than fifteen months. Foxes should live to ten years of age and they have no natural enemies in Britain, yet human persecution and the artificial environment manages to wipe out most of them before they even see winter and spring, rear a family or learn what life is all about.

Looking after orphaned cubs
It may sound as if the lucky cubs are those that are picked up as orphans and taken into captivity by caring humans. Dozens are found each year looking lost and alone, like those little puppies we all dote on. But have these youngsters really been abandoned?

The vixen and her mate, together with their helpers, will make a much better job of rearing a cub than a human can possibly emulate. And at the

Will this cub survive to rear a family of its own

end of their stint they will have a healthy fox family to send out into the world, with none of its wild instincts dulled by the cuddling and petting human foster parents are so good at. I know the future for a juvenile fox may seem pretty grim, but its best chances are with its parents.

There are many published accounts insisting that we 'leave orphaned fox cubs alone'. I heartily agree, but there are occasions when we should intervene, although I must stress only after careful consideration.

Vixens often move their cubs from one site to another. If the cubs are very young the vixen will have to carry them, one at a time, in her jaws. Should dawn catch her in mid-move she may well leave some of the cubs at the old site until the following night. So if you find a cub, or sev-eral cubs, in an earth that is apparently deserted, they should be left alone, at least for the night, to give the vixen time to return and collect them – she will. If she does not return, then some mishap may have befallen her and the cubs do need rescuing and rearing – not a prospect to be taken lightly.

If the vixen moves from one earth to another when the cubs are old enough to walk, they will follow her to the new site but, just like the typical naughty schoolchild, one may stray from the line and be left behind. This little stray is the one that is often spotted sitting in a ditch, calling its sad little bark, all lost and alone. But is it? Once again, when the time is right, the vixen will come searching, homing in on the little bark, scolding the vagrant young-ster and returning it to the fold. That is what usually hap-pens, but if the vixen does not come back for some reason or other, then, and only then, the cub will need rescuing.

The vixen is a superb mother who will do all in her power to keep her family intact. She will always return, if she can. So if you find a family of fox cubs in a barn or an outhouse, under a shed, in a dry drain or even sometimes in a hollow tree, they may well not be deserted. A vixen will often sleep during the day away from her pestering children, just as a bitch will take breaks away from her puppies. It's a wonderful experience to keep watch, from a distance, on a family of fox cubs waiting for the vixen to return. If you haven't got twenty-four hours' worth of patience, then rig up a little indicator such as a single stick over the entrance to the earth, to see if she knocks it away in your absence (of course, you must make sure that the cubs cannot view your ploy or it will become just another one of their playthings). If the vixen definitely does not return within twenty-four hours, the dog fox may try to rear the family, but it will be an uphill struggle for him with no guarantee of success. In this situation I would intervene and take the cubs on for hand-rearing, fully realising that I must do all in my power to keep those cubs completely wild and fearful of people. There is also a system of feeding cubs in the wild.

Of course the loss of one or both parents can have a devastating effect on a family of cubs. But if this situation arises and we are aware of it, we can help out and encourage orphaned cubs to grow in the situation their mother chose for them, within an earth she selected as the most suitable for her cubs.

Cubs will start to venture to the opening of their earth at about four to five weeks of age, usually during the month of May. They will appear fit and playful. Some of the food which the parent foxes leave for them may remain uneaten and scattered around the earth entrance. This should be the scene right through to late July when the cubs may start wandering to fresh sites. During these weeks a careful observer can watch them playing, fighting, or just lying in the sun wallowing in the warmth. At all times they will appear content, alert and healthy.

However, if anything happens to the vixen then the whole situation changes drastically. If the cubs are under five weeks of age then they may be heard whimpering below ground or wandering aimlessly, giving their tiny little barks as a call for their mother. Orphaned cubs of this age will need to be taken away and hand-reared to release in September. But if they are over five weeks old they can be left at the earth and fed throughout the rest of their growing without any need for close human contact.

An earth that has lost its vixen appears a cold, forlorn place. Instead of enjoying a delightful playground, the cubs will be listless and lacking in life, possibly calling for their mother. All the scattered scraps so typical of an earth will now be eaten, scavenged by the starving cubs in a vain effort to stay alive.

If we are completely sure the vixen is gone and that the earth is a safe place, we can help those cubs grow by leaving food around the earth. By the end of May, they will be largely reliant on solid food. In the wild their mother would have provided whole animal food, uncooked, but not necessarily fresh. We should do the same and leave them meat bones, day-old chicks or mice, rabbits and, dare I say it, chicken carcasses. Household scraps and dog biscuit will give the variety their diet needs. But I would avoid tinned dog food as, although nutritious, it does seem to give foxes very loose faeces.

The food parcels can be decreased during July and then, later in the month, the cubs start to move out. After this, sporadic feed supplements will top up what they will then be managing to collect for themselves. By September the cubs will have dispersed, with the vixens probably staying locally and the dog foxes finding themselves new territories elsewhere.

Nature has somehow arranged things so that the stringent defence of fox territories is relaxed from September to December. This, no doubt, allows the juveniles, which are as big as adult foxes, to cross or occupy territories without too much harassment. We should take advantage of this lull in skirmishing to release any cubs that have been reared in captivity during the year.

CHAPTER NINE

GENUINE ORPHANS

Fox cub casualties

Rearing foxes in captivity can be very rewarding but it should never be taken lightly. There are so many pitfalls and mistakes to be avoided that I will only accept 'orphaned' fox cubs at the Hospital if their finders or rescuers can convince me that there was no alternative other than to pick them up.

There are instances where we must intervene to save the cub from a slow death. An injured or sick fox cub may still be nurtured by its parents but they cannot give it any treatment for even simple injuries or illnesses. Therefore I believe that any fox cub that is the victim of a road accident, even though it may not have any apparent injuries, should be taken into care. It may be sufficient just to keep it in for observation for twenty-four hours. Then it can be returned to where it was picked up and observed from a distance as its little barks will probably attract its mother.

A cub that is unconscious or showing signs of concussive injury, such as an inability to stand properly or nystagmus (a flickering of the eyeballs) should be given corticosteroid treatment coupled with antibiotics. It should not be released until it is fully recovered, which usually means that it cannot be reunited with its family. It will then have to be reared until it is old enough for release on its own.

An unconscious fox cub may look to be at death's door but, given the proper treatment for shock, it is more than likely to make a complete recovery. Any fox that does not stand up and flee at your approach should be rescued. A cub sleeping on its side out in the open or under a hedge is sick or injured and needs help.

Similarly a fox cub with an obvious injury, like a broken leg or wound, should be taken in and treated. So should a cub released from a snare. It may develop pressure wounds and should be kept in for some months until it is mature enough to be released on its own.

A few points worth remembering when contemplating taking on a fox cub orphan or casualty are:

1. It *can* and hopefully *will* try to bite
2. It should be handled as little as possible and definitely not spoken to
3. Fleas and other parasites, apart from mange mites, are not a problem and should not be sprayed with insecticides
4. Any animal which cannot use its back legs will probably need to have its bladder emptied manually by gentle squeezing (seek a vet's advice, wear surgical gloves and for more detailed information see my St Tiggywinkles Wildcare Handbook)
5. Foxes do not make good pets and every effort should be made to return them to the wild
6. Foxes should not be allowed to become familiar with dogs
And most importantly,
7. If a cub can be taken back to the place where it was found within forty-eight hours, its mother should return to pick it up. Watch from a distance or a parked car.

Hand-rearing

In spite of all our precautions, our information campaigns and our good intentions, there will be, every year, homeless or orphan fox cubs that need hand-rearing. It really is the most satisfying discipline that you could ever take on. And I do mean discipline, because fox cubs demand a commitment day and night until they are ready for weaning, and then six or seven months' feeding and cleaning followed by the heart-rending release into who knows what. And if you break the rules and end up with a tame fox, you are sentencing it to up to fifteen years' incarceration in your care.

The smallest cubs likely to need hand-rearing could be just one or two days old. They should have some immunity against infection, but if they have fed on their mother's colostrum for at least one day, their immunity is increased. Of course if you are hand-rearing a cub you will not have access to fox colostrum, but goat colostrum would make a good substitute.

Blind, deaf and helpless, this cub is only a few days old

With young cubs of this age, in fact with all rearing of wild orphans, it is absolutely essential to maintain the sterility of your feeding utensils as far as possible. Luckily human babies also demand sterile feeding utensils so most products are easily available from a chemist. Basically the rules are to keep any feeders or utensils exclusive to only one family of cubs. If you find that you are rearing unrelated cubs then use more than one set of feeders and utensils and do not put the cubs together until after they are weaned.

After each feed wash and rinse all feeders and utensils and keep them soaked in a solution of Milton, a sterilising liquid used for human baby bottles.

The first and most important thing to do is to warm the fox cub gradually so that it feels warm to the touch, not hot. A hot-water bottle with a towel around it or even an electric heat pad or an overhead infra-red heater will provide enough warmth, but it is essential that the cub does not get overheated. A complete, safe, heated environment suitable for many young mammals or birds is provided by a Brio Superbrooder (available from Southern Aviaries in Sussex). Provide the cub with a Vet-Bed to keep it dry and snug and, of course, give it a cuddly toy to snuggle up to.

If the cub appears very weak, cold and undernourished, then possibly an injection of warmed dextrose and saline, given under the skin, to about 5 per cent of its body weight, will give it enough strength to suckle from a bottle. Most vets will oblige with this subcutaneous injection of dextrose/saline.

Weighing a cub every day during its stay with you, or at least until you do not need to handle it any more, will give a good indication of its well-being. In the wild, a cub before weaning can expect to grow by fifteen to twenty grams every day. As a foster parent you probably cannot emulate those weight gains but as long as a cub does not lose weight over a forty-eight-hour period it is doing well.

One crucial point that many commentators omit to mention is that very young mammals are unable to urinate by themselves and quickly build up a reservoir of toxic waste products that can lead to fatal uraemia. In the wild

the mother will stimulate her offspring to urinate by lick-
ing its private parts. Obviously I am not asking you to do
this, but any young fox cub needs stimulating by quickly
and lightly wiping a damp cloth or a baby wipe, or even a
dampened cotton bud, back and forth over its urinary out-
let, either its penis or vulva. This needs to be done as soon
as the cub arrives and at least after every feed until you
notice that the cub can manage by itself. However, before
deciding that the cub is managing, do make sure that any
urine passing through the Vet-Bed is not just the overflow
from an over-full bladder but is the result of a conscious
effort to empty the bladder by muscle control. So many
disasters in rearing small mammals have been caused by a
failure to carry out the simple procedure of stimulating the
youngsters to urinate.

Once the bladder has been emptied, the newly arrived
cub should be offered warm fluids by means of a small bottle and teat. Special bottles with a variety of small teats
designed for hand-rearing puppies or kittens are available
in pet stores. Made by Catac Products Ltd, they are literally called 'puppy-' or 'kitten-rearing kits', and are suitable
for use with many small mammals. Another small bottle
and teat set is the Belcroy Premature Baby Bottle which
may be ordered through a local chemist.

Any new cub arrival will be suffering from some degree
of dehydration and even if subcutaneous fluids are not
required its first feed in captivity should still be some form
of rehydrating fluid. All our new arrivals receive Lectade,
available from the vet's or the local agricultural mer-
chant's, warmed to body temperature.

The best way of feeding fox cubs is to stand them on a
towel, or if they are too young for standing to lay them

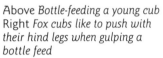

Above *Bottle-feeding a young cub*
Right *Fox cubs like to push with
their hind legs when gulping a
bottle feed*

upright on your lap, and gently press the teat of the bottle
between their lips. At first they may be reluctant to take
the slightly salty Lectade but do not, on any account, force
the teat into their mouths or they may become 'bottle shy'
and always from then on will be difficult to feed. Patience
is the order of the day. But if you have no luck at all, try
mixing the Lectade 50:50 with unpasteurised goat's milk,
once again warmed to body temperature. Shaking a few
drops from the bottle on the inside of your wrist will give a
good indication of whether it is too hot or cold.

Once a cub does start to feed, you can control the flow
by placing your thumb over the open end of the bottle. If
the fluid starts to bubble back out of the cub's nose then
possibly the flow is too fast or the hole in the teat too large.
You have to beware of inhalation pneumonia, where li-
quids get down into the cub's lungs, so if at any time it does
start to cough and splutter remove the bottle and tip the
cub slightly forward until it clears its airways.

Any cub that is settled will probably take the whole

bottle of feed in one go and then refuse a second bottle. This means that as a cub grows it will graduate to larger bottles to satisfy this one-gulp habit of feeding. When it has finished its feed, wipe any excess from around its face with a baby wipe, stimulate it to urinate and, just as you would with a human baby, gently rub its back to release any wind, the air it has gulped down as it suckled from the bottle. Support the cub on its haunches with one hand while you rub its back with your other hand or, alternatively, in true human fashion, hold it upright on your shoulder and listen for the little burps.

The milk we use for rearing fox cubs is unpasteurised goat's milk. Bottled cow's milk is no use whatsoever and if used may even cause digestive problems. To each feed is added just one drop of Abidec multivitamins, available from chemists. There are proprietary puppy-rearing milk substitutes available on the market but the only two we have used successfully for foxes are Lactol, available from pet stores, and Esbilac, a formula milk recently imported from the United States.

Between feeds the young cub should be kept confined in a warm box or cage. A deep cardboard box will do for very young cubs that cannot climb. Of course a Brio Super-brooder provides the security and warmth needed and is easily cleaned. As the cub grows it will need more spacious accommodation, a pen from which it cannot escape. To let a fox cub roam around the house is just asking for trouble, for although you may find it easy to train it to use a litter tray, the cub is always in danger of being trodden on and once it gets its teeth it will start gnawing at the furniture. A Majestic collapsible pen made by Shaws Pet Products of Aston Clinton, Buckinghamshire, can be erected to any size you require and stored flat when not in use. Kiddies' play-pens are not suitable; fox cubs are guaranteed to escape from them and then get into some form of trouble!

Remember, fox cubs are not puppies, they are as agile as kittens and are more adventurous than any other small mammal I know.

After you have put the replete cub into its box, wash and sterilise the feeding utensils and then take a break because the next feed is less than two hours away. Most cubs will let you know by their high-pitched whimpering when they are ready for their next feed. Their feeding regime can be more or less on demand but as a rough rule-of-thumb guide they should be fed every two hours both day and night. As they get older and grow they will take more at each feed, allowing you to stretch their feeding to three-hour intervals. And if you are very lucky and meticulously plan your feeding times, you may be able to get them to sleep through the night and only wake for an early morning breakfast. Keeping them within earshot or rigging up a baby alarm will let you know if they do demand your presence at any time during the night.

A replete cub

The cubs will need their supplementary heating until they are at least three weeks old and their first, needle-sharp milk teeth start to appear. Then is the time to introduce the first solid food, possibly Pedigree Chum Puppy

Cubs grow fast, learning all the time

Food, initially mixed liberally with the goat's milk they will recognise. Keep adding the drop of Abidec multivitamins but also begin to add once a week a pinch of Stress, a calcium and phosphorus supplement designed for growing puppies and available at most pet stores.

This is also the time when your mischievous little cubs will start walking, rolling, swimming and sleeping in their bowls of mushy dog food. It is important to keep wiping the muck off their fur or else they will start to get small sores which are very difficult to clear up.

Once the cubs are about ten to twelve weeks old, try to get hold of frozen day-old chicks or mice to provide them with a more natural complete diet. And, although it may sound gruesome, any small animals or birds freshly killed on the road, or by cats, as this will give the cubs a good grounding in what to expect when they are out in the big, wild world. But you should be careful to check that none of the unfortunate corpses has been poisoned or tainted with other chemicals.

After weaning

As the fox cubs are weaned from the bottle at between four and five week of age, they should not be handled again. In fact now is the time for a single cub to be introduced to other foxes and to start growing up. Cubs have to learn that future human contact will usually spell death and, although I know that it is going to be hard, we as the foster parents now have to frighten the youngsters and loudly shoo them away if they approach us while being cleaned or fed.

At about ten weeks they can go outside and this is where the Majestic pen comes into its own as it can be moved to fresh ground each time the patch it is standing on becomes fouled or dug up. A small tea-chest with no bedding will provide shelter and I like to see cubs with plenty of food and, of course, water at all times.

Fox cubs need the companionship of their own kind

Keeping cubs outside without any human contact will allow their wild instincts to come through, although I doubt if this would be the case with a solitary fox cub. So if you do manage to rescue just the one waif or stray I would strongly recommend passing it on to a wildlife rescue centre that will have a crèche of cubs at various ages. The scaring tactics are against all our human nature but when September arrives and the cubs are due for release they stand a much better chance of survival if they shun all human contact.

Rearing fox cubs demands tremendous dedication and discipline, plus the time it takes to bring the youngsters up to a fit state for release. Even more important, however, is a well-planned and well-executed release scheme.

CHAPTER TEN

BACK TO THE WILD

Release sites

Any releases should be planned meticulously, especially the selection of a fox-friendly site, and preferably followed up by subsequent monitoring of a cub's survival, particularly as completely safe areas are not always available and, in fact, are very rare indeed. An ill-conceived release programme can have a disastrous effect on rehabilitated fox cubs which may find themselves abandoned in the wrong environment.

Even if a site is found that is free from persecution there will always be the inevitable road traffic and other accidental hazards. But these are unavoidable products of the twentieth century that all of us, including foxes, have to live with. The least we can do for any released animal is to minimise the opportunities for danger by picking sites which are as far as possible from motorways or other busy roads and

A recovered fox ready for release

which are free from deliberate persecution by hunters or gamekeepers.

There is not going to be a perfect release site but try to arrange the best possible. And a good public relations programme will calm any people in the area who are uneasy at the thought of having foxes released near them. Their fears are usually based on the myth, or should I say 'mythunderstanding', that blights so many people's attitude to wild animals.

In spite of all the above advice, the most finicky opposition to your choice of site will probably come from the foxes themselves. We, as humans, can have no perception of why a fox chooses its home where it does. Maybe it's for the site's secrecy or seclusion and the available prey. There must be territorial boundaries which are invisible to us, but then foxes in turn seem oblivious to other danger areas and will often set up home on hunting or keepered land, even resorting to the artificial earths which are constructed by some hunts to ensure they always have an animal to chase. The foxes' only concession to these persecutions is to breed more profusely in an innocent, instinctive attempt to keep their numbers viable.

We, of course, can find out where the persecuted areas are and can do all in our power not to release where foxes are likely to be shot, snared, poisoned, or hunted (although the fox may be a little safer on a hunt's land rather than in gamekeepered territory as a hunt is reasonably ineffective at killing adult animals compared with the ruthlessly efficient slaughter carried out by most gamekeepers). Thankfully there are now more and more tracts of land across Britain on which the owners ban all forms of killing. It's not possible to restrict a fox to the safe side of a fence but it is possible to point it in the right direction when it is released.

There are always going to be roads in any district where the release of foxes is contemplated. This, unfortunately, is unavoidable as the only territories devoid of roads, such as the wilderness of the Scottish highlands, or the national parks, have so far proven unsuitable for the released foxes themselves.

Of course if you have your own or a friend's tract of land then instigate the release scheme where there is the least chance of interference. You might imagine that because it is private land you are immune from trespassers who might damage any foxes. This is not necessarily the case but to ensure the maximum amount of protection why not write to local hunts, terrier and shooting clubs and let them know that they are not welcome on your land? Should there be any incursion legal steps can then be taken to ensure your privacy. Nobody has a right over your land except perhaps if there is a public footpath or bridleway crossing it. And even then travellers should keep within the bounds of this right of way.

Looking at present-day fox populations across Britain one can see that more and more foxes are favouring the vicinity of dense human population especially around our larger towns. The foxes of the wilderness country in Scotland and Wales have to work hard to eke out a living and travel vast tracts of land to find enough food. Foxes released in these uninhabited areas have generally failed to survive for long so although it may seem a good idea to pick an area well away from human contact, it probably will not work. Before selecting a site, look to see where other wild foxes live. They know what is best for them, so

as long as you avoid making any releases in the strong territorial periods of mating and cub-rearing (January to
July), any released fox should easily be able to find a
vacant niche where it can settle in.

Foxes are territorial during the mating and breeding season and although most territorial skirmishes are more bark
than bite, the dominant dog fox can inflict serious injury
on a visiting fox. However, as foxes suffer a 60 to 80 per
cent mortality each year there are always vacant territories
for incoming foxes. H. G. Lloyd calculated that even with
a low 33 per cent mortality rate only 45 per cent of fox
pairs would remain intact after a year. This is appalling,
when you think of a fox's dedication to its mate and family. Just imagine how many families are destroyed given
the actual mortality rate, which is much higher.

Preparing cubs for release

For the months prior to release every effort must be made
to ensure that any cubs are quite wild and fully fit enough
to face the rigours of life in the outside world. When an
orphaned fox cub first comes in it may be young enough to
need bottle-feeding, which necessitates the cub being
tame enough to be easily handled. Once it is weaned the
cub should not be handled again and every effort should
be made to make it extremely wary of humans or dogs in
its vicinity. It comes hard to bang on the pen of a cub you
have just reared on a bottle, and at first the cub will be as
distressed as you are – but it must be done. The golden
rules from now on are: no handling of the cub; no talking
to it; no showing it to visitors, and, if possible, do not let it
see you providing the food.

The food at this time should be a menu of what it is

likely to need in the wild. Road-killed casualty rabbits, birds and other animals are eminently suitable and they need not be particularly fresh. Household scraps including chicken giblets or heads will provide a good nutritious meal and will encourage the cub to use all types of food it might find, especially near towns. There is no need to feed it live food as, from about six weeks of age, it will instinctively learn to hunt and perfect the fox pounce which it will practise on dead carcasses.

Much of the learning process is acquired through interplay and squabbling, so it is essential that the lone orphan is intermingled with others of a similar age. Each year many dozens of orphaned cubs are rescued by rehabilitation centres and, as most of these places are full to the gunwales, I am sure that if your facilities were good enough they would be only too happy to pass on two or three cubs to create an ideal crèche for young growing foxes.

To bring the young foxes to the pinnacle of fitness for release they should, after weaning, be housed in a very large pen, at least ten metres by five metres, built in the area deemed most suitable for their freedom. Two-inch-square weldmesh is more suitable than chain-link fencing for the pen construction and it should be wired over the top as well as at the sides because fox cubs prove to be just as agile as a cat in scaling wire fences. It is also worth burying the wire sides to a depth of sixty centimetres to stop the cubs burrowing out before you are ready to let them go. A simple empty tea-chest on its side is adequate housing for two or three fox cubs and can be cheaply replaced. However, an artificial earth in a soil bank will give the cubs a more natural weaning to a life in the wild.

As I have said, do not let them see you providing their food and water every day and, of course, you should not clean them out unless it is really necessary. A good strong hose will generally blast away most waste and, though I hate to say it, will assist you in scaring away the cubs to make them even more wary of humans.

Methods of release

At the beginning of September the door to the cubs' pen can be left open, allowing them to come and go as they please. Keep putting the food into the pen at least until you are certain that none of the cubs is likely to return (they will gradually all disperse into vacant areas).

This method of release is also the preferred system for some adult fox casualties – for instance, where their territory is not known or where there is a chronic history of persecution or disturbance in their original area. Once again, like the cubs, the best time for release is between September and December but this may involve keeping a casualty long after it is healed.

There is always the fear when releasing a fox in a strange area that it may fall foul of the resident foxes. This is particularly true if your released fox is a male – vixens do seem to be more readily tolerated. However, if the fox has to be released sooner rather than later, to establish a pen in the area may enable the local foxes to become used to the newcomer's scent, acknowledge that it has a newly established territory and accept it. Before opening the pen to release the newcomer, secretly observe the area over a few nights to see if any local dog foxes do visit and show aggression towards the captive fox. If they do then it really is advisable to try a pen in a different area, because even

Release a fox where it was found, and if possible, at night

holding the fox until later in the year will cause so much stress to it, and the resident foxes, that a successful release becomes doubtful.

All other adult fox casualties should be released *exactly* where they were picked up. By this I do mean exactly, whether this be on a railway line, in somebody's garden, or, as is often the case with foxes suffering mange, in a garage or a shed. Road casualties should be taken to the place where the accident occurred and there set free sensibly in a nearby field or open area. Keep yourself between the road and the fox but be prepared for it to double back and cross the road, so pick a moment very late at night when there is no likelihood of a sudden car splattering your fox back into care.

Familiar territory is always the most favourable area in which to release foxes because it gives them the best chance of survival, not just in avoiding territorial fights with resident foxes but also in helping them evade the attention of hunters and trappers.

It's never easy to release any fox, especially if you have

grown to know it over a period of time. You wonder to yourself what is going to happen to it. Will it fall foul of a hunter's dog, be trapped in a snare? You can mark your foxes with ear-tags, tattoos, or electronic microchips to monitor their progress. Personally I think they fare much better if they are just given the opportunity to go their own way with no further interference from us, other than the occasional offering of a meal left where they were last seen.

Captivity cases

Some foxes are not likely to survive or to cope at all and these should not be released. In particular I am thinking of tame or imprinted animals which to my mind are incurable and are condemned to a life in captivity. A wild fox with one front leg missing may not be able to cope with all the digging it has to do to find food and create a home. *Old* foxes with worn teeth are probably arthritic and incapable of catching live prey. They would slowly starve if left to their own devices. Lastly, on no account ever release an albino animal of any species. Not only do they tend to be weaker than their normally coloured contemporaries but they often prove to be prime targets for taxidermy as gruesome freaks stuffed to adorn somebody's living room. Just last year two albino fox cubs were spotted above ground for the first time. Within twenty-four hours they had been killed, skinned and prepared for mounting, all before anybody could do anything to protect them.

Releasing Bob

We have recently released Bob, the fox who had lost his tail in a skirmish with a dog. I remember very well how he looked when rescued on the local RAF base: severely injured, suffering from bite wounds and abscesses, and barely able to walk. But, like most wild animal casualties, he quickly responded to treatments and though he lost his dignity as well as his brush, he gained strength and weight and was raring to go.

When I had originally picked Bob up he was limp, lifeless and easily put into a carrying case. Yesterday when I caught him up to take him out he fought like a tiger, making it a tremendous struggle to fold him into the release box. Mind you, it did not help that I had to use a smaller box than usual, since the larger carrying box which we use for the more powerful animals had been dismembered by a badger and was still being repaired.

Bob weighed considerably more than the depressed fox I had originally picked up and he spent the whole journey to the release site trying to dismantle this carrying box. Though I knew he couldn't actually get out, I found myself contemplating with dismay the prospect of having a very strong fox loose in the back of my car, tearing the upholstery in its attempts to escape. Our vehicles are on loan from Toyota, with the provision that we keep them in good condition. My thoughts as I drove down the 'Switchback' (the road towards Wendover where he was to be released) were on how I could explain that the flagship of our fleet, my Land Cruiser, had been eaten by a fox.

I was relieved to reach my destination on the RAF base for the rendezvous with Lisa and David Frost, two of our volunteer team. They lived on the base and had identified a release position in a nearby wood where Bob would have the opportunity to pick up his old haunts.

I let David carry Bob's box, which was just as well as to

reach the release site meant climbing a steep, very muddy hill through thick and very dark thorn scrub. Only with my torch could we see anything in the dark wood but eventually we came out onto a wide, muddy ride and hiked for another mile or so, always uphill, until we were situated high above the tall chimneys of the buildings where I had originally found Bob.

We gathered our breath and then, on a count of three, opened Bob's box. For a fox that had tried to move heaven and earth to escape on the journey up here, he now seemed reluctant to leave and merely stuck his nose out to scent the woodland air. Then, slowly, he ambled out and wandered into the nearest scrub. We could not see him but could hear him in the dense undergrowth. Then as we left and looked back he came back onto the ride.

'Oh, no,' I exclaimed, 'he's going to follow us.'

But no, Bob was just getting his bearings and then, apparently picking up a familiar, but to us invisible, track, he melted into the trees further up the hill.

Our prime objective at the Hospital is to release the patients as soon as they are completely fit, or, as in the case of Bob, superfit, and can re-establish their niches back in the wild. Not only is it better for all these animals to be wild and free but it also takes some pressure off the staff and volunteers who spend every day of the year treating, cleaning and feeding the constant influx of casualties.

Since HRH Princess Alexandra opened the new Hospital in November 1991 the number of animals coming in has increased by 50 per cent to about 15,000 each year. Consequently we have at any one time up to 1,000 patients all demanding attention. The new facilities and the variety of intensive care units make it possible to bring more and more casualties back from the brink, but our success is already putting a strain on the pens and aviaries we had planned to use to cope with any influx.

The foxes and badgers, once they are on the road to recovery, are penned outside in specially made dog pens. Constructed of wood and heavy-gauge wire mesh, these have already been well chewed by the recuperating inmates, each one having been occupied by a constant stream of patients ever since the opening. The fox cubs are penned in larger open enclosures at the end of the run of adult pens, but even these have four youngsters in each pen. The pressure for accommodation at least removes the tendency to keep an animal for too long, but we do have to make doubly sure that each one released is 100 per cent fit.

On the morning after Bob's release, his empty pen has already been cleaned and another fox transferred from intensive care into the open air. The new inmate, a little fox cub called Peter, had had four breaks in a hind leg necessitating surgery and the insertion of various stainless steel devices to stabilise each fracture. In true fox tradition he has healed very quickly, although the leg is still a trifle stiff. The exercise he will get in the pen will ease the leg and there is no reason why he should not eventually be released.

Bob rediscovers his old territory

Chapter eleven

FOXES AND THE FUTURE

Every time I meet a fox I am amazed at the prowess of this animal that so many have ignored or maligned for so long. Just last week I had a rescue phone call from the local council. A fox cub had been spotted walking the parapet of the new multistorey car park in Aylesbury. It was by then, apparently, holed up in a corner on one of the upper floors. This was no place for a fox cub as it was in the centre of the town well away from even a meagre scrap of urban fox habitat, or so I thought. Normally I would leave a healthy fox cub to find its own way home, but it seemed that this one had nowhere to go so I decided to jump into my Toyota 'white charger' and gallop to the rescue.

I had completely underestimated the expertise of even a young fox. When I arrived at the car park and was shown to the upper floor, where the cub was supposedly 'holed up', there was no sign of it. The story I was told was that the car park attendant had called a photographer from the local newspaper, the *Bucks Herald*, who had managed to take a few photographs before the cub had disappeared into a corner. I inspected the corner, and hanging out of the building far above the ground, I found a small hole in

An escaper, four floors up in an Aylesbury multistorey car park

one of the girders that had been used in its construction. This was the only place available for hiding and although it was small, only about fifteen by thirty centimetres (six by twelve inches), I could imagine a small fox squeezing down it. By swinging out over the edge of the building I managed to shine a torch down this small abyss, but could not see the bottom. To assess its depth I tied some bait to a length of twine and slowly lowered it into the hole, hoping any hiding cub would at least snatch at the morsel. Nothing, no signs of life, but at least we could estimate the depth of the hole at about twelve metres (forty feet). The bottom of the girder, which was shrouded in concrete for its full length, was more or less at ground level. If there was a fox deep in the girder, then the only way to get it out would be to smash a hole through the concrete foundations of the car park, a most unlikely solution, though I did suggest it to the borough engineer when he appeared. He was not amused.

I knew if there was a fox in the hole, it would die slowly of starvation unless I could think of some other way out. Before I made any decision or predictions I arranged for some food: frozen day-old chicks were thawed and dropped down the hole on a twelve-metre length of twine. I left this overnight and, knowing any fox's passion for food, reasoned that if the cub was trapped it would at least take the bait.

The following morning the bait was still intact, so I was confident that there was no fox down the hole – but how, then, had it disappeared in that corner, so far above the ground? It must have jumped off the parapet and fallen forty feet to a small shrubbery at the corner of the car park. Was there a dead or seriously injured fox cub hidden in the bushes?

But no. I searched every last inch of the ground-floor area, all to no avail. The cub must have crawled off somewhere, so I spread my search to the nearby railway sidings and the low scrub that lines a nearby brook, one of the many that run through Aylesbury. About fifty metres from the car park I came across a patch of seemingly impenetrable bramble and thicket and as I turned one corner there was a fox cub, presumably my missing fox cub, looking as fit as a fiddle and fleeing into the dense scrub as soon as it saw me. I will never know if that was the cub that had performed the death-defying leap from the top of the car park, but we often hear of cats surviving the most spectacular of falls so why not a fox cub? I continued my search of the surrounding area and found no other signs of a fox cub so had to assume that this survivor was doing very well in its secret thicket in the middle of town and probably made nightly forays into the multistorey car park to pick up unwary pigeons or empty crisp packets. I could only hope that never again would it attempt that leap from the parapet, for if foxes have nine lives like cats, I calculate that it used up all its quota on that first incident.

I often imagine that all over Britain and the rest of Europe many foxes, just like this one, are learning to savour the safety of living in or around the towns and cities. I regularly take part in a phone-in on 'Robbie Vincent's Nightline', a popular programme on LBC, a major radio station which covers London and the south-east of England, and I receive many, many telephone calls about foxes living in the towns and close to people. Some callers have genuine fears about the foxes living under their sheds or visiting their gardens. (They are worried that foxes raid dustbins and tear open rubbish bags, though many films now being made of urban foxes are, once more, proving that much of the fox's reputation is based on fallacy not fact and the culprit is more likely to be neighbourhood dogs and cats.) But more and more people are phoning in to describe the pleasure they get from watching 'their' foxes gambolling in the garden.

With the advent of more access to wildlife through books, films and television, each and every wild creature has its own fan club. Garden magazines are now publishing articles on the virtues of starlings and some slugs; birds like the magpie and crow are being recognised as crucial parts of nature's careful balance; and of course mammals such as hedgehogs, squirrels and badgers are acknowledged to be vital in keeping the countryside viable for us as well as for themselves.

In many publications about foxes there are little snippets describing the benefits they bring to both wild and cultivated areas. There are still conundrums: for instance, why does the Forestry Commission, a public body, spend about £150,000 to £200,000 each year killing foxes? I received this information in a letter from a Forestry Commission representative. Foxes do not damage trees; on the contrary, they help to control rabbits, squirrels and voles which *do* damage trees. And why do many country trusts, now called 'Wildlife Trusts', allow the hunting and shooting of wildlife on some of their reserves? I am confident that these attitudes will alter if only because of the will of the majority of the British public, which is increasing its demands for the protection of all British wild animals.

Mind you, nothing creates more heated argument than the 'great fox debate' and when a Private Member's Bill was put before Parliament early in 1992 by Mr Kevin Mac-Namara MP, the national newspapers and the media carried a rich variety of libel and slander from both sides of the fence. The sad thing is that 'The Wild Mammal Protection Bill' would have given protection not just to foxes but to other vulnerable species like hedgehogs, weasels, voles, moles and many others. Somehow the parliamentary discussions became just another 'great fox debate' and the Bill was lost by a mere twelve votes, no doubt due to the intense lobbying by the British Field Sports Society and the Hawk Board, groups that did not want these mammals to be protected. Sometimes Parliament does not seem to reflect the democratic wishes of the people, as many polls taken at about this time showed the vast majority to be in favour of giving all wild mammals as much protection as wild birds already enjoy. Still it was a small step in the right direction.

Once upon a time the only foxes ever seen were those fleeing from hen-houses or else gibbeted in traps and snares. Now with the increase in wildlife rescue centres and urban fox populations, people are able to see foxes as they really are. I know that any fox we rescue tears at the heartstrings because it is both terrified at our proximity and, generally, so injured that its attempts at escape usually result in a once proud animal dragging itself to its final limits. When we pick up an injured fox it has normally been struggling to survive but has at last succumbed, weak and frail, to its injuries. We cannot console the miserable animal as even a pat on the head or an attempt to stroke its pained body is seen as an aggressive gesture, only adding stress to a fox that is already strained to the limit of its survival. We have to remain detached and administer our treatments as quickly and efficiently as possible, not even talking to the skeletal quivering creature.

However, one or two days of food, warmth and *remote* tender loving care will usually see the fox spitting back in defiance and on the road to a swift recovery and release. This idea of treating an injured fox, or any other wild animal for that matter, is a new concept in the world of conservation. When I first started the Wildlife Hospital in 1978, probably only a handful of people across Europe had the wherewithal to cater for an injured fox, or any other wild animal for that matter. Over the years we have realised that there are literally thousands of wild animal casualties occurring every week and although we already work sixteen hours each day of each week, we could not possibly cope with every casualty. Because of this, we have built at Haddenham, just outside Aylesbury, a wildlife teaching hospital where we can pass on our knowledge and give support to others who want to devote their lives to wildlife casualties. I say 'devote their lives' because looking after wild animals can never be a nine-to-five job and is well outside the scope of groups or individuals who want to work to a clock. But I think that even before we start up the courses at our teaching hospital, we will have already saved the lives of many foxes by our advice lines and our information literature. In particular we have shown that sarcoptic mange can be cured – previously it was considered untreatable and any fox suffering from it was killed. Now the simple injectable cure is readily accepted and available and it is being widely used to the benefit of many suffering foxes.

I have two mange-affected foxes in the Hospital at the moment. One is a small cub which was brought in the day before I wrote this; flat out, emaciated and intensely miserable. As usual we set up a transfusion of fluids and complementary drugs via an intravenous drip and overnight the cub has bucked up and eaten two bowls of food, her intravenous drip and the plastic collar we put on to protect it. This morning she is up on her feet and threatening to devour any jailer who tries to recover the remnants of the effective mange treatment equipment.

The other fox was one caught about five weeks previously. He was curled up, exhausted, close to death, on the lawn of an impressive house overlooking the pretty village of Aldbury, in Hertfordshire. He seemed oblivious to the dinner party taking place on the patio and even ignored the lady of the house stroking him. It was this concerned lady who had called us in the first place and I assured her that the fox would be released back onto her lawn once he was fit. After all, this was a superb place for a fox to live, especially with all the hand-outs after dinner parties.

He has now received our standard first aid and routine treatments for mange and, just five weeks later, has an almost full coat and is almost fit. Today we placed him in an outside pen to harden him off after his five weeks of luxury living in our heated ward for large mammals.

The aim of our courses is not to replace the veterinary profession whose members, although they receive no training with wild casualties, have an important role to play in the diagnosis and treatment of diseases and injuries. The courses are designed to provide knowledge of the four facets of wildlife care which are generally outside the scope of the busy veterinary practice: rescue, first aid, post-treatment convalescence and release,

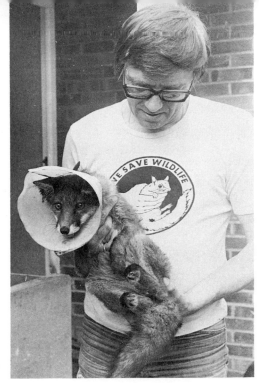

Vix, one of the first foxes ever treated at the Hospital, never accepted confinement

all of which are within the capabilities of anyone wanting to help wildlife. We have established a Code of Practice which has been greeted by the veterinary profession as a good working arrangement between their members and wildlife rescue units, and we have just staged the first congress for those who have taken up the Code of Practice. These people, collectively, have become known as the European Wildlife Rehabilitators' Association.

We are also now seeking to establish a vocational qualification in wildlife care and to develop it as a profession in its own right, with possible job opportunities as the number of rescue centres grows.

Our prospectus for the courses was recently launched

Above *Baldric, the fox cub who turned out to be a dog*

Left *Noddy led a brief but happy life at the Hospital*

for us by the Minister of State for the Environment and Countryside, Mr David Maclean MP, who reiterated the need for wildlife rescue centres and qualifications to bring relief to the millions of wildlife casualties across Europe.

As I look out of my study window at the full fox pens, brimming over with the life and excitement of growing fox cubs, I remember some of my early foxes. Vix, who just would not settle in the enforced confinement needed to repair a leg shattered by a snare. Noddy, an unfortunate fox cub whose congenital deficiencies caused him to hop rather than walk, with a constant nodding of the head. And Baldric, a supposedly very sick fox cub found on the Watford bypass – who

turned out to be a very old, small dog. Baldric is still living in our home four years later, and still gets mistaken for a fox cub by those who do not know him.

The foxes in the pens below me now are completely wild. When I release them, they will not look back and say, 'Thank you' – and that's the way it should always be.

USEFUL ADDRESSES

Department of the Environment
Wildlife Division
2 Marsham Street
London SW1P 3EB

The Fox Project,
11 Caistor Road
Tonbridge
Kent TN9 1UT

League Against Cruel Sports
Sparling House
83–7 Union Street
London SE1 1SG

MAFF
Ministry of Agriculture, Fisheries
and Food
Whitehall Place
London SW1A 2HH

Poisons Hotline 0800 321 600
(freephone)

**National Society for the Abolition
of Cruel Sports**
Secretary: John Docherty
9 Medway Drive
Forest Row
East Sussex RH18 5NU

**New Forest Animal Protection
Group**
PO Box 45
Ringwood
Hants BH24 2NL

NFBG
**National Federation of Badger
Groups**
c/o John Taylor
16 Ashdown Gardens
Sanderstead
South Croydon
Surrey CR2 9DR

Shaws Pet Products
50 Weston Road
Aston Clinton
Bucks HP22 5EL

Southern Aviaries
Tinkers Lane
Hadlow Down
Uckfield
East Sussex TN22 4EU

**The Wildlife Hospital Trust
St Tiggywinkles**
Aston Road
Haddenham
Aylesbury
Bucks HP17 8AF

BIBLIOGRAPHY

Anderson, M.D., *Animal Carving in British Churches*, Cambridge University Press, 1938

Bang, P. and Dahlstrom, P., *Animal Tracks and Signs*, Collins, 1972

Blackwood, C., *In the Pink*, Bloomsbury, 1987

Bryant, J., *Hunts, Source of Killer Disease* (Wildlife Guardian, Spring 1992), League Against Cruel Sports

Churchward, R.A., *A Master of Hounds Speaks*, National Society for the Abolition of Cruel Sports

Cruel Sports, Number 20, Winter 1986, League Against Cruel Sports

Dahl, R., *Fantastic Mr Fox*, Puffin Books, 1988

Dyce, K. M., *Textbook of Veterinary Anatomy*, W. B. Saunders, 1987

Ginsberg, J.R. and Macdonald, D.W., *Foxes, Wolves, Jackals, and Dogs*, IUCN, 1990

Harris, S., 'Distribution of the Suburban Fox', *Mammal Review*, Vol.7, No.1, March 1977, Blackwell Scientific Publications

Harris, S., 'The Food of Suburban Foxes with Special Reference to London', *Mammal Review*, Vol.11, No.4, December 1981, Blackwell Scientific Publications

Harris, S., *Urban Foxes*, Whittet Books, 1986

Harris, S. and Macdonald, D., *Orphaned Foxes*, RSPCA, 19..

Harrison, D. L., *Mammals of the Arabian Gulf*, Allen & Unwin, 1981

Hewson, R., *Victim of Myth*, League Against Cruel Sports, 1990

Lloyd, H. G., *The Red Fox*, Batsford, 1980

Macdonald, D., *Running with the Fox*, Unwin Hyman, 1989

Macdonald, D., *The Encyclopaedia of Mammals:1*, Allen & Unwin, 1984

Macdonald, D., 'Waiting for Rabies', *BBC Wildlife*, June 1988

Macdonald, D., *Rabies and Wildlife: A biologist's perspective*, Oxford University Press, 1980

Ovsyanikov, N., 'The Odd Couple', *BBC Wildlife*, Vol.8, No.11, November 1990

Pastonet, P. P., Brochier, B., Thomas, I. and Blancou, J., *Agriculture: Vaccination to Control Rabies in Foxes*, Commission of the European Community, 1988

Perry, R., *Wildlife in Britain and Ireland*, Croom Helm, 1978

Potter, Beatrix, *The Tale of Mr Tod*, Warne, 1988

Roberts, J. J., *Up Against the Law, Animal Rights & the 1986 Public Order Act*, Arc Print, 1987

'Seeing in the Dark', *Wildlife Publications*, May 1979

Stocker, L., *We Save Wildlife*, Whittet Books, 1986

Stocker, L., *The Hedgehog & Friends*, Chatto & Windus, 1990

Stocker, L., *St Tiggywinkles Wildcare Handbook*, Chatto & Windus, 1992

Sumption, K. J. and Flowerdew, J. R., 'The Ecological Effects of the Decline in Rabbits due to Myxomatosis', *Mammal Review*, Vol.15, No.4, December 1985

Thomas, R., *The Politics of Hunting*, Gower, 1983

Turbak, G. and Carey, A., *Twilight Hunters*, Palace Press, La Jolla, 1987

Vesey-Fitzgerald, B., *Town Fox, Country Fox*, André Deutsch, 1965

White, T. H., *The Book of Beasts*, Jonathan Cape, 1969

Wistar Institute, *Guard Against Rabies*

INDEX

Bold indicates pictures

Aesop 15
Alopecia 15
Ancestors 31
Aristotle 17

Badger 18

Calls 50
Canidae 29
Casualties **93**, 96, 100, **102**,
137, **165**
Cub-hunting 76
Culpeo 33

Disease 118, 125
Dogs 11
Dusicyon 33

European Wildlife
Rehabilitators
Association 165
Euthanasia 99
Eyes 54, **54**

Faeces 56, **56**
Family life 51, 130, 150
First Aid 103, 106
Fleas 20, 21
Fox - Arctic 29, 31, 45, **46**
- Azara's 34
- Bat-eared 29, 35, **36**
- Bengal 47
- Blandford's 48
- Cape 49
- Common 34
- Corsac 31, 48
- Crab-eating 34
- Cross 44
- Culpeo 34
- Fennec 29, 37, **37**
- Flying 32
- Forest 34
- Grey 40, **40**

Fox - Hoary 35
- Island Grey 40
- Kit 38, 39
- Pale 49
- Red 29, **30**, 41, **43**
- Rüppell's Sand 29, 48
- Samson 14
- San Joaquin kit 39
- Silver **44**
- Silver backed 49
- Simien 32
- South American grey
34
- South American Red
34
- Swift 39, **39**
- Tibetan sand 48
- Vinegar 33
Fox cubs 2 ,3, **6**, 11, **11**, **12**,
25, **52**, 80, 126, **128**, **131**,
132, **133**
Fox on stilts 33
Foxproofing 68, **68**
Fox shark 32
Fractures 101, 104, **105**, 114

Garden Foxes 73, **73**, 75
Grasper 18

Handling 18
Hearing 53, **54**
Hedgehog 16
Hunting 82

Lambs 64, **65**

Mange 46, 107, 121, **123**,
164

Orphans **78**, **127**, 133, 139,
139, **142**, **144**, **145**, **146**

Pelage 14, 60

Physiologus 19
Pliny 17
Plutarch 17
Postage stamps **26**, 27, **28**
Prey 59, 61

Rabies 125
Release **10**, 147, **147**, **153**,
157
Rescue 92, **101**, 158, **159**
Reynard the fox 21, **22**, 23,
27

Samson fox 14
Scent 55
Shock 14
Skeleton 30
Snares 18, 88, **89**, **90**, 119

Teeth 29, 59, 112, **113**
Territory 71
Tracks 19, 58, **58**

Vermin 24
Veterinary treatment 99, 111,
115, **116**, 120
Vulpes **18**, 19, 31

Weight 60

Zorro 33
- Azara's 34
- Crab-eating 34
- Grey 34
- Sechuran 35
- Small-eared 34
- Small-hoary 35